supported by

action
planning
let's start from here

# the good guide
# to working with
# Consultants

by Jon Fitzmaurice and Jenny Harrow

# NCVO Good Guides

Written by leaders in their field, NCVO Good Guides are accessible guides to good practice for organisations working in the voluntary and community sector. Other titles in the series include:

- The Good Trustee Guide
- The Good Financial Management Guide
- The Good Management Guide
- The Good Campaigns Guide
- The Good Membership Guide

For more information about the Good Guides and the complete range of NCVO titles, go to www.ncvo-vol.org.uk/publications or phone NCVO's HelpDesk free on 0800 2 798 798.

Members of NCVO receive a 30% discount on all titles, and membership is free for organisations with an income of less than £10,000 per year. To find out more, go to www.ncvo-vol.org.uk/membership
or ring our Membership team on 020 7520 2414.

Published by NCVO
Regent's Wharf All Saints Street London N1 9RL

First published 2003
This edition published 2007

© NCVO 2007
Registered Charity Number: 225922

Designed by NCVO
Typeset by JVT Design
Printed by Latimer Trend and Co. Ltd

British Library Cataloguing in Public Data
A catalogue record for this book is available from the British Library

ISBN: 978-0-7199-1664-9

Every effort has been made to ensure the accuracy of the information contained within this Good Guide. However, NCVO cannot be held responsible for any action an individual or organisation takes, or fails to take, as a result of this information.

# Authors

Jon Fitzmaurice
Senior Visiting Research Fellow and Independent Consultant at
Agents For Change

Jenny Harrow
Professor of Voluntary Sector Management, Centre For Charity
Effectiveness, Cass Business School, City University

The CASS Business School's Centre For Charity Effectiveness
(www.centreforcharityeffectiveness.org) has a team of consultants offering affordable advice and help in a wide range of areas
that affect organisational effectiveness, performance improvement and change management.

The idea for the guide arose from pre-consultancy work undertaken by the Centre For Charity Effectiveness during 2005/6 with
the 20 organisations wishing to explore social enterprise as a way
forward. The project was facilitated by City University's Centre
For Innovation Transfer, which secured funding from the Higher
Education Innovation Fund.

## Acknowledgements

The authors wish to acknowledge the help and assistance
received from Mariana Bogdanova, Jean Barclay, Margaret
Bolton, Denise Fellows and Greg Campbell.

We would also like to thank those colleagues who contributed
insight boxes and case studies.

iv

# Contents

# Sponsor's Foreword

You may have come across the following definition of a consultant – someone of whom you ask the time; they ask to borrow your watch, tell you the time, then steal your watch.

There is an important lesson hidden within this cynical, if not entirely inaccurate, definition: you the client already had the watch; the role of the consultant was to draw this to your attention, and to help you come up with the answer. But it was perhaps unnecessary for the consultant to steal the watch!

I have always been firmly of the view that the best consultants don't have all the right answers. They have all the right questions. You, the client, know your organisation much better than I do. You are more committed to it. You are the one who is going to have to make things happen when I have moved on to the next client.

So why do you need me, the consultant? Because you want someone with that external perspective, that willingness and ability to ask searching questions; you want someone without all the 'baggage' who can help focus on the problem or opportunity in hand, and identify a way forward.

This concept of 'a way forward' is an important one. The Action Planning logo of a simple pile of stones is known as a 'waymark' – something that has long been used to identify a path or route. When we engage with a client we do so as fellow travellers on a journey.

We recognise that one client's starting point may be different from another's, and that while the consultant's familiarity with the route is a great advantage, each client will want to make the journey in their own way, and at their own pace. Our role is to make that journey as straightforward and comfortable as possible.

Action Planning is delighted to support the production of this NCVO Good Guide. We believe passionately in the importance and effectiveness of the sector in tackling so many of the issues facing the world today. We believe that consultancy can play a valuable supporting role if used appropriately, and we commend this book to you as a helpful guide to making sure that you get the right help at the right time from the right person.

Now, does anybody want to know the time....?

**David Saint**
**Chairman, Action Planning**
**www.actionplanning.co.uk**

**action planning**

let's start from here

# Move forward with Action Planning

As a leading consultancy to the not-for-profit sector, we have helped hundreds of organisations to raise capital and revenue funding, recruit key people, and plan ahead. We work alongside our clients, helping each to make the journey in their own way, and at their own pace. All of our consultancy staff have senior-level experience, and work as a team to deliver practical solutions to client needs.

We provide a combination of advice and 'hands on' implementation for capital appeals, revenue fundraising and bid writing, research, management consultancy and recruitment for senior posts. We work closely with ACEVO and key funders to organise the largest UK events for not-for-profit sector leaders.

Our job is to help organisations succeed in situations where they are struggling due to a shortage of skills or capacity or both. If you are facing such a situation, do get in touch - in confidence, and with confidence.

*"Action Planning gave sound advice which has enabled us to move faster than we had hoped. The right level of support focused on the right outcomes was what we wanted, and that's what we got."*

**Richard Lloyd, Director General, Consumers International**

**Call 020 8642 4122** now for a discussion without obligation, or visit our website **www.actionplanning.co.uk**

Action Planning, Mid-Day Court, 30 Brighton Road, Sutton, Surrey SM2 5BN

strategy and fundraising consultants

# Introduction

Consultants can provide a cost-effective way of meeting needs that are beyond your in-house resources. They can be expensive – both in terms of their fees and your staff time in working with them – so it is important to take care in planning any consultancy assignments.

This guide is intended to help organisations in the voluntary and community sector select and make the best use of the right consultant for each assignment. Used correctly, consultants can resolve difficult issues, help organisations access funding and bring new ideas and insights. Used incorrectly, they can demotivate staff and place a drain on what are already limited resources.

## Who is a consultant?

Consultants are entrepreneurial project-based workers who advise or support an organisation in order to achieve change. Usually they focus on a particular aspect of change, in a time-limited context.

Consultants are expected to offer qualifications and abilities that come together to provide expertise of a wider or more specialist kind than is normally available within a single organisation. This is of prime importance when an organisation is seeking to identify, initiate and then implement change of some kind, whether technical, behavioural or organisational.

Consultants may bring very specific kinds of expertise (for example, project management, facilitation of mergers) or generalist expertise through experience in the particular sector. Consultants may work on one single project as a contractor to 'get the job done', or they may work on projects simultaneously and have multiple or several clients at any one time.

In either case, bringing this expertise to an organisation is likely to be costly. A consultant is usually sought to bring particular and often new kinds of value to the organisation.

Management consultancy has been defined as 'the creation of value for organisations through the application of knowledge, techniques and assets to improve performance' (Management Consultancies Association).

Measuring the 'creation of value' is not always easy. But this dimension keeps the question of 'why use a consultant' very upfront – what is the added, or more importantly, the distinctive value a consultant can bring to an organisation that your own people cannot?

Finally, consulting is a human activity – interpersonal relations are therefore a central feature of understanding what consultancy is.

## The growth in management consultancy

Within the private sector the use of consultants is well established and continues to grow. The Management Consultancies Association estimates that the UK consulting industry is currently worth just over £10.1 billion per year. More recently, both the public and voluntary sectors have come to use, and sometimes even rely on, assistance from consultants with increasing regularity. The Association estimates that spending on consultants in the entire public sector is around £2 billion. Professor Ian Bruce from Cass Business School estimates that the voluntary and community sector is spending between £30 and £50 million per year on consultancy services.

However, it is a largely unregulated industry and it can often be difficult to ascertain who would be the best person for the job. Also, employing a consultant can often be costly. It therefore needs to be approached carefully.

## How to use this guide

This guide will help you to:
- prepare for recruiting a consultant
- plan what you want your consultant to do
- select the right consultant for your particular assignment
- brief and formally engage a successful consultant
- manage the ongoing relationship with your consultant.

Appendix 1 provides a useful checklist that summarises the stages set out in this guide so that you can take a step-by-step approach to commissioning a consultant.

This guide is intended to be used as a reference into which you can delve, as and when necessary, to find advice and guidance. Don't feel you need to read it from cover to cover!

# 1 Why, when and where to use a management consultant

This chapter looks at what management consultants are good at and where and when to use them.

What consultants can offer an organisation
- Additional/distinctive knowledge
- Additional skills and experience
- Independence/neutrality
- Personal style and outlook

Making use of consultants' expertise
- Analysing and developing strategy
- Process management
- Facilitation/mediation
- Passing on knowledge and experience
- Providing extra capacity
- Resolving governance issues

Kevin Curley, Chief Executive at NAVCA (National Association for Voluntary and Community Action) says that 'local voluntary organisations, frequently strapped for cash, are understandably reluctant to hire consultants. But if an initial investment results in a more coherent strategic plan or a more persuasive project proposal it will be money well spent.'

## What consultants can offer an organisation

If consultants are deployed in the right way in your organisation, then they can be invaluable. They can bring:

- additional/distinctive knowledge
- additional skills and experience
- independence/neutrality
- a helpful personal style and outlook.

### Additional/distinctive knowledge

Usually you'll be looking for someone who has knowledge you need to utilise. This may be based around particular issues, such as finance or IT, or around specific sectors in which you work, such as health, training or conservation.

Either way, you'll be looking for someone who knows more about some aspect of your work than anyone you currently employ. He or she will also need to be able to make use of that knowledge to address whatever problems you face, and/or to implement an action plan or recommendations that your organisation has accepted.

Often consultants will list a wide range of tasks that they are willing to undertake. However, it's obvious that they will know more about certain areas than others. Don't be afraid to establish exactly what they know and the extent of their experience.

---

## How to retain knowledge gained by consultants

Depending on the assignment, your chosen consultant may spend a good deal of time accumulating new knowledge on your behalf. In these circumstances it is important to ensure that, when he or she completes the project, your organisation has retained the information that you paid your consultant to find out about.

It should be possible to achieve this by agreeing with the consultant in advance that the assignment will include documenting background information that will not necessarily appear in the final report or alternatively simply passing it on to another member of staff.

Fundraising and membership research assignments are examples of where this could arise:

- Fundraising: If an assignment revolves around identifying new sources of funding, then the consultant may be involved in exploring various avenues and in making numerous new contacts. Some, or many of these, may not figure in the final report or recommendations, but should nevertheless be passed over to the organisation.
- Membership research: Similarly where research is carried out into the existing membership or into new membership services, there may be a significant amount of information gleaned from members that does not fit into the final report but which an organisation would want to capture for future use.

### Additional skills and experience

As well as additional knowledge you will almost certainly be looking for someone who has extra 'know-how' and experience.

This will have been acquired over a period of time and will be rooted in the experience that the consultant has gained from past employment and previous assignments. It may be issue- or sector-based, or a combination of the two.

This is an important part of what you will be paying for. It will underpin the consultant's ability to understand your organisation, to apply their knowledge to best effect, to anticipate and resolve unexpected problems and to skilfully handle interpersonal relationships. It will also enable your consultant to put the organisation's performance or problems into a wider context.

Running an organisation is tiring and sometimes it can be difficult to 'see the wood for the trees'; this may be the case for both staff and committee members. A good consultant can draw on new perspectives and insights gained from past experience and challenge any aspects of the status quo that may be standing in the way of progress and change.

Consultants are often used to help with difficult human resources (HR) issues, such as redundancies or industrial tribunals. As well as having the requisite knowledge of legislation and procedures, they also need to have first-hand experience of these scenarios in order to avoid potentially time-consuming and costly errors.

Consultants' expertise can also be used to ensure prudent behaviour from an organisation where considerable risk is involved, for example, where there is insufficient in-house experience of borrowing or investing money. You should ensure that consultants are not used by staff to abdicate responsibility for a particular course of action. If this is the real reason for bringing in a consultant it raises questions about the legitimacy of the expenditure and also perhaps about the ability of staff to do their jobs. Under these circumstances senior management, or trustees where senior staff are involved, should examine the competence of staff.

### Independence/neutrality

Consultants can offer an independent and neutral perspective. Because they are outside of the organisation and its hierarchy they are well placed to:

- help deal with difficult or sensitive issues, while remaining unaligned with any particular part of the organisation
- bring an intellectually neutral perspective to bear on issues.

However, for this to succeed consultants need to be perceived as independent and neutral rather than having being brought in to protect or promote a particular interest. For this reason the method of appointment is often crucial (see Chapter 5). Any assignment concerned with reorganisation that might lead to loss of jobs or redeployment is an obvious case in point.

### Personal style and outlook

A consultant's personal style and outlook manifests itself in an ability to sympathise with the aims of the organisation and to get on with, motivate and energise members of staff.

While you can set out to objectively assess a consultant's knowledge and experience, and be relatively sure of their independence and neutrality, it will be more difficult to assess their ability to deliver this 'added value'. Nevertheless, depending on the assignment, this may turn out to be something on which your organisation places a very high premium.

Figure 1: What a consultant offers to a client

## Making use of consultants' expertise

Before you select your consultant you need to be clear about the nature of the task and what is required. This section briefly examines a range of different activities that consultants are called on to undertake, which include:

- analysing and developing strategy
- process management
- facilitation/mediation

- passing on knowledge and experience
- providing extra capacity
- resolving governance issues.

Clarity about exactly what you want done will help in selecting someone with the appropriate expertise.

### Analysing and developing strategy

A good deal of higher order management consultancy involves dealing with change by analysing complex problems and making recommendations for action. These assignments might include technical issues, such as choosing an IT system for a growing organisation or devising a fundraising strategy, or management issues, such as business planning or how to respond to changes in the external environment.

These are by nature higher order issues and will call for a relatively high level of expertise from a prospective consultant.

---

### A selection of consultancy tools

This box sets out some of the tools that a consultant might use to analyse and diagnose organisational issues and problems.

#### SWOT analysis

This involves carrying out a review of an organisation in relation to four distinct areas: its 'strengths', its 'weaknesses', the 'opportunities' upon which it could capitalise and the 'threats' that it faces. The resulting picture is then used as a basis for generating further analysis, leading to recommendations.

#### PEST analysis

This is another technique used to gauge an organisation's prospects, but focuses more on external factors, namely: political, economic, social and technical.

#### Matrix analysis

This is a graphical technique: competing options or products are set out along a vertical axis and compared against a selected number of factors/features along a horizontal axis. For instance, different ways of restructuring an organisation could be compared in terms of how they score in relation to different factors such as overall cost, number of redundancies and so on.

---

**Process management**
From time to time your organisation may need to manage a particularly complex process requiring a combination of knowledge and experience that is unavailable from within the staff team. In these circumstances it makes sense to take on a consultant to oversee what needs to be done.

Examples of this include managing the merger of two organisations, introducing a new finance system and implementing a set of recommendations relating to a reorganisation or a redirection for the organisation.

## Using a consultant to manage change

Community Action Network, one of the UK's leading organisations for the promotion, networking and direct support of social entrepreneurs and social enterprises, decided in 2004 that it needed to transform. The world had moved on since CAN's inception six years earlier, and in many areas CAN had achieved its stated goals.

We recognised that a first step in moving forward would be to review, and if necessary rewrite, CAN's vision, mission and values. CAN engaged an award-winning 'user-centred' consultancy to work with a broad range of stakeholders, including senior managers, staff and trustees. This was well received as the consultant listened, empathised, proposed, facilitated and visualised (rather than bullying and being macho!), all of which helped us to deal with complex issues in a constructive and supportive fashion.

The goal was to make the transformation of CAN as transparent, inclusive and apolitical as possible. More than anything, we wanted to take people along with us, rather than have to persuade them later.

The outcome from this exercise was a revitalised and refocused CAN. With a renewed vision, mission and purpose in place – and with a clearly understood set of values – business clarity emerged.

**James Alexander**
**Former Managing Director, CAN**
**www.can-online.org.uk**

### Facilitation/mediation

Sometimes the neutrality and independence of consultants are as important as their knowledge and experience. This is the case when consultants are called in to work with groups of people or individuals to identify how to handle change or resolve individual differences.

Many organisations use a consultant as a facilitator when faced with difficult decisions that need to be resolved between different stakeholders, for example, decisions about future strategy and developments involving both staff and trustees.

A similar role arises where an outsider is needed to mediate or arbitrate between conflicting individuals or groups. This could arise where a chief executive officer (CEO) and chair of an organisation are in conflict or where members of a management team are in dispute.

---

## Using a consultant as a facilitator

ChangeUp gave us a rare opportunity to employ a consultant to assist us in modernising the way in which the two CVS (Council for Voluntary Service) in the Harrogate district work together.

The consultant spent time early in the project listening carefully to staff from both organisations. She impressed everyone with the way she took time to understand the perspectives of individuals and also our different cultures and ways of working. Staff found it easy to trust her as a neutral, but interested, person.

The consultant facilitated two lively staff away days where she used her expertise in facilitating groups and also her experience of a range of different group exercises to generate ideas and develop the bonds between us. Having an external consultant for these events meant everyone could relax without feeling responsible for the success of the days.

The directors of the two CVS also met regularly with the consultant to develop the joint strategy and action plan for the future. New ways of working are often challenging but she kept us on track with her straight-talking but approachable manner. Making time to do something extra is sometimes difficult in small organisations, but she gave

continued...

---

us the motivation to commit to developing the plan so that we ended up with a sense of shared ownership and commitment to ways of working together.

The consultant's view was that two ingredients for successful partnerships are mutual trust and a shared vision or commitment. We already had those ingredients, but by working with an expert facilitator our shared values became more explicit and we were able to see more and better ways of working together, for the benefit of the local voluntary and community sector.

**Hazel McGrath**
**Director, Harrogate and Area**
**Council For Voluntary Service**
**hazel@harrogate.org**

**Passing on knowledge and experience**

Consultants are frequently asked to pass on their specialist knowledge and experience, and this can take place in a number of contexts:

- Training and development: Many consultants offer training as one of their services and run courses for groups of people or sometimes even for individuals.
- Coaching: This is where a consultant is brought in to work with an individual in relation to a specific issue or problem, usually for a limited period. For instance, it could take the form of working with a new manager to develop her or his management skills or helping an experienced manager deal with a new project.
- Mentoring: This is also a one-to-one relationship but it is intentionally less specific and the consultant usually works with the individual over a longer period of time and attempts to pass on a range of knowledge and experience or skills. Because of the open-ended nature of mentoring, care needs to be taken to ensure that both parties remain focused with regard to what exactly it is that the relationship is supposed to achieve. A good example of this would be where a consultant works with a new chief executive across a whole range of issues arising from his or her job.
- Twinning: An alternative to paying a consultant as a mentor could be to set up a twinning arrangement. This involves two people from different organisations, who are often senior managers or CEOs and operating in different sectors (for example, voluntary sector and private sector), entering

into what is intended to be a mutually beneficial relationship. In practice there may be some mentoring involved if one party turns out to be more experienced than the other, but it is intended to be a two-way relationship. There needs to be clarity and a mutual understanding about what each person wants to get out of the relationship. In the absence of this, it can become unfocused and drift. Organisations such as Business In The Community host twinning programmes.

## Using a consultant as a facilitator

As the new director at Quaker Social Action, I needed to write a strategic plan. This wasn't something that I had done before and I was apprehensive about committing a lot of time and energy to such a process if I got it wrong.

I decided to engage a consultant to advise and coach me. I wanted someone to support me to develop and implement the process of putting the plan together, as well as offer me advice on the content. For me, this was an exercise in skill development and also in creative problem solving, so it didn't make sense to outsource the work.

The key to the success of this consultancy would be my ability to relate well to the consultant. Therefore, unlike other times when I have engaged consultants, I didn't put it out to tender, but considered a few consultants I knew and with whom I felt I could work closely. This led to a direct approach to one consultant.

The result? We worked together for several months. We delivered the strategic plan bang on target and I was extremely pleased with it.

The reason? The consultant I chose was someone I could work with and I think we shared a value base that built a good foundation. I felt that we had similar ways of communicating and managing to reconcile differences of opinion constructively. I felt that she allowed space for me to grow; she did not seek to stamp her ownership on the finished product but rather created opportunities for me to find my way.

**Judith Moran Director**
**Director, Quaker Social Action**
**www.quakersocialaction.com**

## The value of mentors

I have had a mentor for three years and as a result I would be slower to buy additional consultancy services. A mentor should not be used to replace, or as a substitute for a consultant; but if all is going well, a mentor can build your professional confidence and encourage you to be resourced from within.

My mentor was arranged by New Philanthropy Capital, which manages the service, and we either meet or spend an hour on the phone about every six weeks. He has had a career in investment banking and was looking to increase his involvement in the voluntary sector. The professional mentor can do all of the following:
• be a sounding board, a mirror, a coach and an interpreter
• grow an understanding of you and your organisation over time
• be objective, but on your side
• spot your strengths and weaknesses
• grow a professional relationship of trust, but not from a financial base
• be a resource of good contacts or a good textbook
• be available in a crisis.

They should not be used as:
• an extra member of staff
• your fundraiser
• a trustee.

I have found that my mentor has given me 'permission' to use my personal gifts and resources as the leader of Dreamscheme.

**Kate King**
**Director, Dreamscheme Network**
**www.dreamscheme.org.uk**

**Providing extra capacity**

There are a variety of situations in which your organisation may need both extra capacity and the expertise that a consultant can deliver. These include:

- Working on a short-term assignment: This might be where you need additional capacity from someone with higher-order skills and experience, but only for a very limited period, which rules out a temporary appointment.
- Preparing a last-minute bid: An opportunity may arise to put in a complex bid for a valuable contract, but there may be no one immediately available to undertake the necessary work. In this situation, buying in expertise may prove very cost-effective if the contract can be won.
- Working on a regular but occasional basis: This may be appropriate where you have an ongoing need for higher-level skill or experience but assistance is required only for a limited time each week or month. In these circumstances a part-time appointment might be an option. However, if a consultant has extra experience and skill, they might be able to do the job in less time and possibly to a higher standard. For example, many smaller organisations deal with the media from time to time but don't have the resources to create a separate public relations (PR) post. Using a consultant within a limited budget can be an effective way of securing continuity together with a high level of expertise.

**Resolving governance issues**

Consultants can help with problems relating to governance. This is a particularly sensitive area and so you should recruit a consultant who can draw on a depth of knowledge and experience in relation to governance issues, and who can facilitate difficult discussions from an independent standpoint.

Among the most common assignments are those dealing with:

- trustee board size/structure/subcommittees
- division of responsibility between staff and trustees
- board/executive representation on board
- trustee/board recruitment/remuneration
- trustee/board performance.

## Reviewing the role of the board

Action for Kids (AFK) had just appointed several new trustees and wanted to ensure that they and the existing trustees all had a common understanding of governance and its application to AFK. Staff from Action Planning were engaged to facilitate a governance training day, which entailed an assessment of the board, its role and composition. They decided that an external facilitator would be able to help the board through an honest self-assessment and identify gaps in the overall understanding of the governance model.

The one-day session started with a self-assessment quiz to test the trustees' knowledge of the ideal roles of the board, chief executive and senior staff. The questions were phrased in a light-hearted way, and the answers used as talking points to explore how the governance model should work. Even the experienced trustees found that they had some misunderstanding regarding roles and responsibilities. For new trustees, at least one of whom had not served on a board before, it provided a clear foundation.

Following the self-assessment, the trustees discussed the way the board had functioned in the past and how it would need to work in the future in order to appropriately support the kind of organisation that AFK planned to be. The trustees identified areas for development and assigned responsibility to specific people to move these forward.

Although AFK is a very well run organisation, staff found it helpful to have external facilitation for this session because the consultant was able to highlight misconceptions and knowledge gaps, as well as ask tough questions about tricky issues such as term limits and skill sets. This allowed the board to reflect on areas for improvement.

**Cynthia Hansen,**
**Director of Management Consultancy, Action Planning**
**www.actionplanning.co.uk**

# 2 Alternatives to using a consultant

This chapter looks at the pros and cons of alternatives to using a management consultant.

Internal staff resources/internal secondment
Committee or board member
Pro bono assistance
Secondment
Interim appointment

It is worth pausing to consider whether or not you really do need a paid consultant for the assignment you have in mind or whether there might be another less expensive but equally effective option available. These include making use of:
- internal staff or creating an internal secondment
- a committee/board member
- pro bono assistance
- a secondment
- an interim appointment.

## Internal staff resources/internal secondment

Sometimes it may be feasible to use an existing member of staff with the necessary expertise to take on an assignment. However, for this to work she or he will obviously need to have the required knowledge, experience and skills, and it must also be possible to release this staff member from his or her existing job or to secure the necessary cover to free them up.

| Possible pros | Possible cons |
|---|---|
| • **Cost:** no fees, but there may be associated costs if temporary staff have to be taken on to provide cover for the secondee <br><br> • **Commitment:** likely to be high, since the secondee may well see it as a chance for career development <br><br> • **Knowledge of the business:** likely to be very good, which reduces the need for other staff to become involved in briefing someone coming in from outside | • **Disruption to the organisation:** the secondment could disrupt the smooth running of the organisation and result in additional unanticipated expenditure <br><br> • **Lack of expertise:** the individual may not be able to bring to the assignment the same degree of expertise as an external consultant <br><br> • **Loss of independence:** there would be an inevitable loss of neutrality/independence <br><br> • **Conflict of interest:** it's possible that, depending on where they come from within the organisation, there could be some sort of perceived conflict of interest |

## Committee or board member

Sometimes you may find that you have a suitably qualified board member who is in a position to undertake the assignment in question.

He or she is likely to have a thorough understanding of your organisation and what is required. However, such an appointment needs to treated with caution. As the group of people ultimately responsible for the governance of the organisation, board members have a vested interest and therefore cannot provide the neutrality and independence that comes with an external consultant. This means that there will be a variety of circumstances where a conflict of interest might be perceived to arise and lead to a board member's analysis and recommendationsbeing seen as partial.

| Possible pros | Possible cons |
|---|---|
| • **Cost:** the work should ordinarily be undertaken on a no-fee basis, otherwise consideration should be given to employing an external consultant – however, there might be circumstances in which a heavily discounted fee could be paid, except in the case of regis- tered charities, which are not legally permitted to pay board members in this way<br><br>• **Commitment:** could be expected to have a high degree of commit- ment to the organisation and the assignment<br><br>• **Knowledge of the business:** depending on extent of their previous involvement, they should have a good grasp of your business | • **Conflict of interest:** there could be a possible conflict of interest if, for instance, the assignment was to do with governance<br><br>• **Lack of independence:** as the 'employer' there's a danger that the individual concerned would be perceived as being partial and not independent<br><br>• **Knowledge of sector:** may understand the business but be relatively unfamiliar with the sector – could then be difficult to refuse once started<br><br>• **Redress:** little scope for redress if their advice proves incorrect or inappropriate (for example, choice of IT system or accounting package)<br><br>• **Blurring of responsibilities:** could lead to a blurring of responsibilities between staff and committee that might cause problems after the assign- ment was finished – but it could also provide a board member with greater insight into the organisation<br><br>• **Time:** as with any volunteer there is always the danger that they will have difficulty fulfilling the assignment, given their other commitments – need to take a view |

## Pro bono assistance

Pro bono assistance comes free, or at least heavily discounted, from professionals who should be able to provide whatever expertise you require. However, the fact that you're not paying for it doesn't mean that it should be treated differently from any other assignment. The consultants involved should be offering you the same service as they do to their regular clients and you, as the client, should commit yourself to the assignment in the same way as if you were paying the bill.

As ever, the challenge is to identify what exactly is available and how to access it, within the time frame to which you're working.

Some companies independently provide pro bono assistance to voluntary and community organisations, often as part of their CSR (corporate social responsibility) programme. Quite frequently these are large commercial firms, such as management consultants, accountants, lawyers, HR specialists and PR companies, but there will also be many smaller firms and individual professionals willing to provide pro bono assistance. In these instances you will need to approach them directly.

Another route is via one of a number of organisations that have been set up specifically to broker pro bono assistance, sometimes but not always in relation to a particular profession. These include ProHelp, a network of over 1,000 professional firms run by Business In The Community and administered by 40 different groups around the country (see Appendix 6).

| Possible pros | Possible cons |
|---|---|
| • **Cost:** this would normally be undertaken at no cost, but on occasion some firms ask for nominal payment, often to try and ensure that the relationship is conducted on a professional basis | • **Knowledge of the business:** will they understand your business, regardless of how high powered they might be? |
| • **Access to expertise:** it may be possible to secure the services of a highly skilled person – more qualified than you would normally be able to afford | • **Appropriate experience/skills:** because the consultancy is free it may be difficult to ascertain whether they have the correct skills in the same way that you would in the case of someone you were paying, and you may have no say in who is made available to assist you |
| • **Access to additional resources:** as part of the arrangement it may be possible to secure access to other resources to which the in-dividual providing the consultancy can call upon – in the case of a large business this could be valu-able and take various forms: use of their facilities for meetings or away days, access to training courses relevant to your staff and even help from other members of staff | • **Problems with deadlines:** will they have the time to do it and keep to your deadlines? |
| | • **Indemnity insurance:** will you be indemnified against bad advice? |
| | • **Reputational damage:** if they default, it could affect your rep-utation – both parties have a vested interest in the relationship being conducted on a professional basis and for this reason it may be sensible for a simple agreement to be drawn up that sets out each party's responsibilities and mutu-ally agreed deadlines |

## Pro bono – a provider's view

Pro bono help is a great way of getting expert advice or specialist skills for organisations on a low budget. If you're 'shopping' for pro bono support don't be tempted by every offer that crosses your desk: think carefully about who will best provide the service you need – just as you would if you paid for the service.

The Cranfield Trust offers support through projects with a defined objective – for example, to prepare a strategic or business plan, to set up a job evaluation scheme or to help with designing a feasibility study for a new trading venture. Careful planning is really important since working with any consultant, paid or pro bono, takes time and effort and so, although there's no charge, there are still resources involved.

At the outset, clients submit a proposal to the trust which is followed by a visit from one of our project managers. We then work with the client to prepare a project brief, taking the view that good diagnosis of the problems or issues to be resolved is an important part of the consultancy process. We match the project to a volunteer consultant with appropriate skills from our register of managers from the commercial sector, and carefully brief him or her so that time with the client is useful from the start.

We know from our client feedback that pro bono support can get great results and really help client organisations achieve change – free!

**Amanda Tincknell**
**Director, Cranfield Trust**
**www.cranfieldtrust.org**

## Getting pro bono help to develop a business plan

Lazarus Environmental, a recycling and waste management community organisation, received pro bono professional support from a local firm of accountants via ProHelp.

It provides invaluable waste management and environmental projects to the local community in a highly deprived area. It needed assistance with developing a business plan to help it apply for much needed grant support. The aim of the business plan was to help Lazarus Environmental apply for funding to expand its operation. This expansion involved purchasing larger premises to allow it to provide more extensive facilities to unemployed people, asylum seekers and the wider community of Heddon-on-the-Wall and the east end of Sunderland.

ProHelp appointed BKR Haines Watts to the project and a member of its team set about developing a detailed and professional business plan. The project was in two phases – once the business plan had been prepared, the firm went on to help Lazarus develop its financial systems.

Chris Jones, Lazarus Environmental's Project Manager, was delighted with the result. He said, 'The business plan prepared by Haines Watts is excellent and it will be instrumental in levying essential grant support for the expansion of our organisation.'

**ProHelp**
**c/o Business In The Community**
**www.prohelp.org.uk**

## Secondment

Another option is to try and secure a secondee from an organisation with suitable skills and experience, but at no cost to your organisation. However, you should bear in mind that it's unusual for arrangements of this nature to be put in place very quickly.

Since the organisation providing the secondee has to have the necessary resources to allow someone leave of absence, the most common secondments tend to be between the commercial and voluntary sectors. However, there are instances of secondments taking place between two voluntary sector organisations, though it is usually from a larger to a smaller organisation.

Secondment opportunities are usually made available either to staff interested in career development or to those who are nearing retirement, but how they are set up varies considerably. Sometimes they are organised in such a way that the secondee is available continuously over a period of time, perhaps for three, six or even twelve months. On other occasions, the secondee will continue in his or her existing post and will be made available for a specified number of days or weeks which will be spread over an agreed period. Depending on the assignment, either arrangement can work well.

| Possible pros | Possible cons |
|---|---|
| • **Cost:** the arrangements relating to secondments do vary, but it's common for the organisation actually seconding the individual to continue to pay their salary | • **Lead in:** it could take a long period, perhaps several months, to identify a suitable secondee or for someone suitable to become available |
| • **Long-term assistance:** a secondment could turn out to be quite a long-term arrangement, possibly three, six or even twelve months – where this is the case one of the major attractions is the extra capacity that the secondee brings with them | • **Mismatch:** the skills/experience and knowledge of the individual on offer may not match those you would ideally like in a prospective secondee – however, if it's largely a question of knowledge, then given sufficient time this can be acquired |
| • **Access to additional resources:** it may be possible to strike up a relationship with their parent company and gain access to other resources (for example, facilities or training courses) | • **Understanding of your business:** where a secondee is coming from a very different environment he or she may find it very difficult or even impossible to understand your business and/or the sector in the time available |
| | • **Commitment:** you need someone who is committed to undertaking the assignment and who is not being 'off-loaded' prior to retirement |

## Interim appointment

It might be possible simply to recruit someone on a temporary contract in order to undertake your assignment. Where it's primarily a question of additional capacity that is needed, rather than higher-order expertise, this may be a good alternative. It may also be possible to make a part-time appointment.

However, you'll need a flexible recruitment policy to enable you to recruit at short notice. If your recruitment procedures prevent this you may need to review your recruitment policy.

| Possible pros | Possible cons |
|---|---|
| • **Cost:** by taking on an interim employee you can avoid having to pay someone at a consultancy rate<br><br>• **Availability:** as an employee he or she is likely to be available for more time and can be more easily directed to do exactly what your organisation wants | • **Delay:** it may take too long to arrange<br><br>• **Abortive recruitment:** you could end up failing to recruit and lose money as a result of recruitment costs<br><br>• **Knowledge retention:** you may lose information/knowledge from the organisation because the person you have employed is only on a temporary appointment |

# 3

# What type of consultant is right for you?

This chapter looks at how different types of consultants operate and how much they cost to help you decide which one might be best suited to your circumstances.

Types of consultants
- Freelance consultants
- Dual interest consultants
- Sector-based not-for-profit consultancy networks
- Sector-based commercial consultancies
- Generic commercial consultancies

How consultants charge
- What is included in consultants' daily rates
- Types of payment

How much do good consultants cost?

## Types of consultants

Consultants work in different ways – these include:
- freelance consultants
- dual interest consultants
- sector-based not-for-profit consultancy networks
- sector-based commercial consultancies
- generic commercial consultancies.

### Freelance consultants

There are many consultants operating within the voluntary sector who work alone as sole traders. From time to time sole traders may collaborate with other consultants and even refer to one another as 'partners' or 'associates'.

Associates are freelance consultants who:

- collaborate informally from time to time with other freelance consultants
- work regularly with others on a formal basis in some kind of partnership, often using the word 'associates' in their business name
- work as contractors for another consultancy.

It's worth being clear about the status of the person who may be working for you, especially if you're dealing with a large firm of consultants, since it might have implications for the relationship between the consultant and her or his employer.

You also need to be confident that associate consultants have been carefully selected and vetted by the organisation employing them, and that their work is well managed and monitored.

| Possible pros | Possible cons |
|---|---|
| • **Distinctive expertise:** you can choose a consultant with the specific area of knowledge and experience that you are looking for and know that he or she is the person with whom you will be working | • **Range of expertise:** you'll have access to only one consultant – if the assignment requires a range of expertise some of it may be outside her or his particular areas of knowledge and experience |
| • **Transaction costs:** you'll be dealing with only one person and therefore communication should be straightforward and uncomplicated | • **Capacity:** there will be limitations on the amount of work he or she can undertake, which could potentially limit the individual's availability – at worst your consultant could become over-committed |
| • **Overhead costs:** these will be lower than those of consultants who have to maintain office premises and staff – ordinarily their fees could be expected to reflect this | • **Professional development:** your consultant may not have access to other colleagues with whom to discuss problems or seek advice and may not have the time or resources to keep up with latest developments |

## 'Start-up' consultants

You may come across individuals just starting out as consultants. Some of these will be people who are very knowledgeable in their field, have a high degree of expertise and who have decided to move into consultancy as a career move. Others may have struggled in their previous employment and are turning to consultancy as a means of trying to find work. In these latter circumstances, you may not want to be the organisation that finances their ascent on a new learning curve!

If you do come across individuals who are new to consultancy and who you are interested in employing then examine their CV carefully, find out the circumstances in which they left their previous employment and take up references, including one from their last employer.

### Dual interest consultants

These are people undertaking consultancy as part of, or in addition to, their other paid employment. They could be academics, journalists or professionals. This is an arrangement that could work out very well in the right circumstances, but it's important to be clear about their status before you engage them.

| Possible pros | Possible cons |
|---|---|
| • **Expertise:** it's possible that the knowledge and experience that dual interest consultants possess as a result of their other paid employment could make them ideal to undertake certain tasks | • **Capacity:** dual interest consultants may have commitments arising from their other paid employment which could pose problems in relation to their ability to deliver |
| • **Reputation:** they may have a reputation to maintain, outside of their consultancy work, and therefore will be anxious to ensure that their work is of a high quality | • **Status:** it's important to confirm that they're permitted to undertake freelance work and that there is no risk of their being prevented from completing the assignment |
| • **Back-up:** if they are associated with a well-resourced organisation then you may be able to take advantage of this | |

**Sector-based not-for-profit consultancy networks**

There are a variety of organisations that host networks of consultants working on a not-for-profit basis or who are government funded. This is usually undertaken as one of a number of services that they provide to a particular sector or constituency. Examples of these include Solace (Society of Local Authority Chief Executives), CAF (Charities Aid Foundation), Community Matters, The Digbeth Trust, Neighbourhood Renewal Unit (neighbourhood renewal advisers) and PrimeTimers.

Each network will have a number of freelance consultants on its books working as associates. Once a request for assistance has been received, it will either direct the client to a suitable consultant or ask several consultants to put forward their CVs and give the client a choice. Quite often the contract for the consultancy will be between the organisation hosting the network and the client, rather than directly with the consultant. In addition, the terms and conditions, including the daily rate, will usually be determined by the host and therefore there will be no need to negotiate these with the consultant.

Usully the client has to pay for the consultancy in the normal way (lthough it's likely that the charges will be lower), but there are a limited number of schemes where the consultant's costs are met from grants or other sources and there is no charge to the client. However, where this is the case, organisations wanting to secure the services of a consultant usually have to make an application and, as with any scarce resource, not all applicants will succeed (see Appendix 6 for details of these networks).

| Possible pros | Possible cons |
| --- | --- |
| • **Cost:** where there is a charge the service is likely to be less expensive than a comparable commercial consultancy <br><br> • **Range of knowledge and experience:** the consultants working for the host organisations are likely to have been recruited on the basis of their specialist knowledge and experience of the area in which the network operates. <br><br> • **Quality control:** where the network is well-managed by the host organisation, there should be clear criteria for accrediting new consultants, a proper induction process and procedures for managing and monitoring performance <br><br> • **Professional development:** a good network will take steps to make some sort of investment in the professional development of associates | • **Quality control:** there could be a danger that the organisation running the network may not have sufficient resources to organise proper accreditation of new associates and adequately monitor and manage the performance of its associates <br><br> • **Lack of control over choice of consultant:** the client should always be able to choose between consultants, but there may be a limited choice |

## Not-for-profit network: CAF Consultants

CAF has been running a network of consultants for more than 15 years and currently has 40 associate consultants based around the UK. The quality of the consultants on CAF's network is a high priority and they are selected through a formal interview process which includes references and a probationary period. We select consultants via a range of criteria including their location, skills reflecting the consultancy services offered by CAF and experience of consultancy within the charitable sector. Most importantly, we have learned from our customers what is required from a consultant and have adapted our recruitment processes accordingly.

*continued...*

Once on the network consultants are offered regular update sessions from CAF and our partners, which give them learning opportunities that directly benefit their charity clients and their own personal development. Recent examples of contributors to consultants' sessions include Open University, Ethical Property Foundation and Charity Finance Directors Group.

In addition to meeting up, the CAF consultants benefit from a virtual network which allows them to share information with each other outside of face-to-face sessions and is their source of information both about CAF and the work opportunities available to them.

Organisations coming to CAF are offered consultancy through two routes: either via our grant programme or fee-based consultancy. Whichever route they choose we offer the same quality of service, including a choice of consultants, project management by CAF staff and quality control on all consultancy reports.

Consultants are monitored during the consultancy via CAF staff and, once the consultancy has been completed, via feedback forms from the organisation. This information is regularly reviewed and relates directly to the consultant's retention on the CAF network, thus giving CAF's consultancy clients confidence in the quality of our network.

**Claire Crump**
**Grantmaking and Consulting Manager, CAF Consultants**
**www.cafonline.org**

## Not-for-profit network in action: business expertise from PrimeTimers

Green-Works, a major social enterprise success story, recycles office furniture for reuse in charities and has seen its turnover rise from £2,000 when it was founded in 2000 to £2 million in 2006.

As a new and rapidly expanding social enterprise it has needed to use a variety of professional and business services. These include accountancy, marketing, operational and business planning, and management training.

Colin Crooks, Founder of Green-Works, says that, 'Time and time again PrimeTimers has found the right person for us, someone that not only has the technical skills and experience – after all you would expect that – but someone who fits with our ethos, culture and the characters in our team.'

With PrimeTimers you get top-level experience and talent at an affordable price that will assist you with a specific project and help you to build your organisational capacity by enabling you to capture the learning skills within the business.

In return, we give people working with PrimeTimers from the commercial world an ideal chance to dip their toe in the water of the charity sector to get an introduction to its culture and ethos, to benefit from our extensive network of contacts and to learn a completely different approach to management and how different organisations measure performance.

A word of advice – think through what you want a consultant to do and clearly define the project and your expectations. The better defined the brief, the better results you will get – if you are vague it will not work as well and you will have wasted a great opportunity.

**Alison Yoe**
**Membership Manager, PrimeTimers**
**www.primetimers.org.uk**

## Sector-based commercial consultancies

There are many commercial firms of consultants that specialise in working within the voluntary sector and often have particular areas of expertise – such as health, housing or childcare – or particular specialisms, such as funding, organisational reviews or IT. They may be quite small or employ as many as 20 or 30 people and often are led by someone who previously worked within the sector before starting out on a freelance basis and subsequently growing the business.

Their staff may be employees, associates or a mixture of the two – whatever their status, you should establish who you are dealing with and their relationship to the firm.

| Possible pros | Possible cons |
|---|---|
| • **Distinctive expertise:** small consultancies will understand the environment within which you work and your business<br><br>• **Quality control:** if they are well run then you can expect them to monitor the work of their consultants<br><br>• **Range of consultants:** they may have access to a range of well-qualified and experienced consultants | • **Overheads:** compared with freelance consultants small consultancies may carry more overheads and be somewhat more expensive, but this does not automatically follow<br><br>• **Quality control:** if they use associates and don't recruit or manage them well enough then this could be a problem |

## Generic commercial consultancies

These are often larger commercial consultancies offering 'generic' management consultancy on strategy, organisation, technology and operations, as well as a variety of specialisms, to the business community at large. The top end of the market includes leading private sector firms such as Price Waterhouse, Accenture and Deloitte.

Broadly speaking, the larger the firm the more expensive it is likely to be. Unless it has set up a specialist arm (such as Accenture's not-for-profit Development Partnerships section, which works with overseas development agencies) the company will probably have limited knowledge of the voluntary sector, despite its other attributes. However, there may be occasions when you would consider using them, for example, when sufficient funds are available or when a large consultant's brand of expertise is required. Examples include public housing and health where complex financial modelling is required in advance of bidding for contracts.

| Possible pros | Possible cons |
| --- | --- |
| • **Range of knowledge and experience:** firms employing large numbers of people should be able to draw on a wide range of knowledge and experience from among their consultants<br><br>• **Back-up:** large firms will have well-staffed offices providing back-up to their consultants<br><br>• **Monitoring and evaluation:** you can expect work to be automatically monitored and evaluated by the firm – where there is a hierarchy of consultants within the firm, the more junior consultants should be supervised and overseen by more experienced senior members of staff<br><br>• **Professional development:** provision is likely to be made for professional development across the whole organisation | • **Cost:** the cost of running offices and employing administrative staff will be passed on to you as a client – large firms offer what they consider to be a premium product, which by nature is very expensive<br><br>• **Lack of control over choice of consultant:** this will not always be the case, but for larger assignments they may assign a team of consultants to each project (some of whom may be fairly junior) and therefore you may have limited choice over who you work with<br><br>• **Lack of experience of the voluntary sector:** the majority of their work is likely to be in the private sector and therefore they are likely to have had little experience of the voluntary sector – large firms will tend to make light of this, but it may be that you need assistance from consultants who understand the environment in which you and your particular business work |

## The impact of ICT on consultants

Computers, and in particular the internet, have revolutionised the way in which many consultants work:

- Research: ICT has transformed consultants' capacity to carry out research and means that what might previously have taken days or even weeks if information was difficult to obtain can be undertaken in a matter of hours.

- Intranets: Large firms can now run intranets that enable them to keep their employees in touch with one another at any time of day or night and share information in a secure setting. This means that employees have continual access to what is in effect a virtual office.

- Extranets: Associate consultants can work together through the medium of an extranet that is capable of providing all sorts of opportunities for collaboration and exchange of information across a network of otherwise unconnected individuals.

- Overheads: ICT is of particular help to individual consultants and has helped to create a more level playing field between individuals and those consultants operating with the benefit of additional staff. It has made it possible to cut down on overheads without compromising the ability to deliver a good service.

- Access to information about consultants: ICT also makes it possible for clients to research consultants via their websites and to access information about them that would previously have been unavailable (see Chapter 5).

## Networks Online

Networks Online runs a set of overlapping extranets which provide confidential and secure online facilities and a range of shared core services (for example, Experts Online) for organisations wanting to network their members, users or associates.

Each network is branded to match that of the host organisation that is buying the service and is accessed via the organisation's own website.

CAF consultants (see the box 'Not-for-profit network') use Networks Online to create a virtual organisation. This enables their associate consultants to communicate with CAF and each other, and have common access to a range of shared information.

Networks Online provides members with:

- email and webspace
- advanced group working facilities
- searchable member profiles
- technical support
- added value online services (for example, Experts Online and the Xpress regeneration and funding news service)
- searchable information resources (for example, funding and good practice).

**Simon Berry**
**CEO, Ruralnet UK**
**www.networksonline.org.uk**

## How consultants charge

There is no fixed formula for how consultants charge, but usually they hire out their services on the basis of an hourly or daily rate. However, the daily rate charged by consultants can vary between a few hundred pounds a day in the voluntary sector, to thousands of pounds a day in the higher reaches of the private sector. Because of this variability, it's important to try to understand how these amounts are calculated.

### What is included in consultants' daily rates

Consultants' fees may seem expensive when compared with what employees are paid. However, they need to build into their fee a variety of costs including:

- taxes: whatever they charge will be subject to taxation
- overheads: the cost of running an office and possibly employing support staff
- 'down time': an allowance for holidays and sickness since, unlike employees, consultants don't get holiday or sickness pay
- pension and insurance costs: consultants need to cover themselves in these areas – in addition, many clients will require consultants to carry public liability insurance, employer's liability insurance and professional indemnity insurance
- professional development: the cost of time spent developing their professional knowledge and keeping up-to-date with best practice
- unremunerated work: the cost of preliminary work with clients, prior to being commissioned, which on occasion may be aborted – where a consultant bids for work in competition with others this will almost always be 'at risk' (that is, they will not be able to recoup the costs of bidding – which can be quite substantial in the case of a major project – and will often not win the work).

Businesses with a turnover in excess of a prescribed amount (currently £61,000) are obliged to charge VAT. If you are registered for VAT then it's possible to reclaim what you've paid. If you are not registered, then this will simply amount to a surcharge on the price of the assignment. In this latter circumstance it is important to work out what VAT liability may arise in connection with the contract and factor this into the overall cost.

It is common for consultants to charge expenses (for example, travel or accommodation), but it's important to make sure that these are properly documented and fall within parameters that are agreed before the assignment commences. In some cases, for example, where you are seeking a fixed price quotation, you may want the consultant to include her or his anticipated expenses costs. Some consultants may choose to incorporate expenses within their daily rate. For certain items you may wish to cap the potential costs, for example, stipulating a limit on the nightly cost of hotel accommodation.

In addition to the above, some consultants will also factor in an amount that they will treat as profit that accrues to the practice or company and is allocated, perhaps annually, to senior partners and/or shareholders.

Finally, regardless of the so-called on-costs above, bear in mind that it's not realistic to compare consultancy rates with the costs of employing staff. As Greg Campbell from Campbell Tickell Associates points out, 'When a client brings me in for a job, they aren't simply buying my time on that day; they're paying for twenty years of experience. It's not like employing a member of staff. There's no waiting for three months before somebody gets their feet under the table, and then another three months before they're producing useful outputs. I'm expected to get on and deliver results.'

**Types of payment**
It is important to understand how consultants charge out their time in order to ensure that you are getting value for money.

Variable fee assignments
The most common arrangement is to pay for the hours or days actually spent by the consultant(s) on the assignment. This means that it will be important to establish the basic rate paid in respect of each consultant's time, which may differ where more than one individual is involved. You will also need to find out if there are differential rates used to cover evening and weekend work (though this would be unusual) and travelling time, which should count as 'down time' and be charged accordingly, if at all.

Fixed fee assignments
An alternative arrangement is where there is a fixed fee, agreed in advance, for the assignment and it is up to the consultant to undertake the work within a set number of days or hours.

For the client this has the advantage of effectively transferring risk to the consultant and also allowing the organisation to know the final cost in advance. However, under these circumstances it's always possible that the consultant will take a cautious approach and overestimate the amount of hours or days needed in order to guard against running out of time.

Payment by results
A third, less common, way of charging is for the consultant to work at risk and be paid solely on the basis of results: either a flat rate fee or a percentage. Where this does occur, it's most likely to be in the case of assignments that result in the organisation making a financial gain such as securing a grant or a new contract.

Professional bodies such as the Institute of Fundraising require their members not to undertake work on this basis since they believe that it is at odds with good practice (for example, it discourages investment in longer-term relations with donors), The Charity Commission also has concerns about this method of payment. However, there may be occasions when there are no other alternatives and it is the only way to engage external assistance.

### Bonus payments

Sometimes agreements are made to pay the consultant a bonus in recognition of a successful outcome or if the project is completed ahead of schedule. Arrangements of this nature need to be approached carefully and require considerable clarity.

In such a case, it may be that the consultant's daily rate would be lower than he or she would normally receive.

---

## Negotiating a fixed price

You have a limited budget, so is it possible to get a consultant to give you a fixed price instead of having to deal with the uncertainty of being charged by the hour or day? This is a classic dilemma. Some consultants are happy to quote a fixed price but others are reluctant, depending on the kind of work. Understandably, the consultant does not want to do unpaid work, while you want to pay only for time actually spent working.

The root of the problem is uncertainty – not enough time spent at the outset reaching a genuine mutual understanding of what needs to be done and how long it will take. The solution lies in breaking the work down into clearly understood logical chunks. If both of you can agree on what needs to be done then the consultant will be less worried about doing unremunerated work and you can decide whether the result is worth paying that much for.

Although there are exceptions, most projects can, and should, be broken into pieces. In fact the bigger and more complicated the project, the greater the need to carve it up. Without a clear understanding of the elements of the work you have no hope of controlling any consulting contract that is longer than a few days.

**Graham Duncan**
**Independent consultant**
**Formerly Director of Lending and Development,**
**Charity Bank**

## How much do good consultants cost?

This is the question to which everyone wants an answer. No organisation wants to pay more than is necessary or feel that it was overcharged.

There's a huge variation in what is charged between individual consultants, between firms of consultants and even between consultants within the same firm, and so it is impossible for a guide of this nature to attempt to set out any sort of scale of fees. However, it is possible to give some indicative guidance relating to the range of charges that exist (accurate at the time of writing – 2007).

Consultants operating in the voluntary sector invariably charge upwards of several hundred pounds a day, but the exact amount will depend on the task, the firm, the consultant and the location. At the lower end of the market you might expect to pay around £250–350 per day for a freelance individual, but the fee may be two or even three times this amount if you go for a very experienced person or for someone who works for a consultancy with additional overheads. A figure around the middle of this range (that is, £350–£550) is not an unusual daily rate for an experienced consultant, but £1,000 a day is no longer uncommon.

Not surprisingly, consultants in the private sector tend to charge rather more. Their lowest fee is likely to be the median voluntary sector fee and it's quite common for large firms to regularly charge out staff for twice or three times that amount. Fees for senior project managers and partners can be expected to be well in excess of this.

However, you should always bear in mind that consultants are sometimes willing to charge less to a client whom they think has limited resources or where the assignment is of such interest that they're simply willing to work for less. Remember this and don't be afraid to ask at the outset about the 'scale' against which you're being charged. Needless to say, you also need to be clear about exactly when you start to pay and when the assignment ends.

If you are in doubt about whether or not you're being asked to pay too much, then talk to NCVO members in your area to find out about their experiences.

## Preliminary discussions with consultants

When do consultants start charging for their time? There's no one answer to this question, but it should always be possible to talk to consultants about a possible assignment, or even meet up with them to do so, without incurring any costs. Consultants recognise that some of their time will be 'at risk' and they tend to build into their fees time spent talking to prospective clients.

That said, you need to make sure you're clear about when the clock starts ticking and this wouldn't usually arrive until they have been formally commissioned, unless by prior arrangement.

# 4 Drawing up the brief for a consultancy project

This chapter sets out how to draw up the initial brief for a project and specify what expertise you need from the consultant.

Who is in charge?
- Client-led
- Consultant-led

Identify what you need
- Consult on what needs to be done

Prepare a brief
- Statement of outcomes for the organisation
- The assignment
- Outputs
- Methodology
- Management arrangements
- Timescale
- Budget

Presenting versus underlying problems

For a consultancy assignment to be successful, it's important to be clear about what exactly you want the consultant to do and what qualities you are looking for.

## Who is in charge?

Consultancies can be 'led' by the client or the consultant. In reality many consultancies are neither entirely client nor consultant led, but fall somewhere in between.

### Client-led

In this scenario you have a clear view of the stages you need to go through in order to achieve your desired outcome and the brief for the consultant will be fairly prescriptive.

However, this is not the same as when the recommendations/outcomes are already known and the consultant is being used to deflect possible criticism or deliver what will be perceived as unpleasant news, for instance, where a restructuring is being proposed that would result in redundancies.

### Consultant-led

In this situation you know the outcomes you want to achieve (for example, the consultancy will lead to the organisation being able to set up an affordable and effective management structure) but need guidance or specialist expertise in getting there.

## Identify what you need

### Consult on what needs to be done

You need to set out what the organisation wants to achieve and what you want the consultant to do in pursuit of this. Depending on the assignment this could be something quite detailed or a fairly short document.

Your own department may be able to determine what goes into this initial brief if the assignment is straightforward – for example, developing a training package. However, there will be other circumstances when there needs to be some form of consultation within the organisation about its content. For example, if the consultancy assignment will affect the future direction of the organisation then it will be important to get staff signed up to what is being proposed.

#### Consultation with staff

If you decide to go down this route then you need to take a decision about which staff members should be consulted. Not only will this assist in getting the objectives right, but it will help to get other staff committed from the very beginning and ensure that there is an adequate degree of ownership.

#### Consultation with trustees

Sometimes it will also be appropriate to consult with the trustees or board members. This would be the case where the brief dealt with governance or the overall direction of the organisation.

## Prepare a brief

The result of these consultations then needs to be set out in writing. The length and amount of detail required will vary depending on the nature of the assignment.

This will provide an internal document that will underpin the consultancy and to which staff and trustees can subsequently refer. This could be very useful in the event of any problems or disagreements arising in the future in relation to what had been intended or agreed. It will also act as the basis for setting out exactly what prospective consultants will be asked to address (see Chapter 5) and for agreeing final instructions with the chosen consultant (see Chapter 6).

### Statement of outcomes for the organisation

There needs to be a clear statement that sets out the changes being sought within the organisation so that everyone can be clear about what sort of assignment it is appropriate to ask a consultant to undertake. For instance, your organisation may have identified that it wants improvements in its financial management systems.

### The assignment

This will be dictated by the outcomes that have already been identified and will be the task given to the consultant to undertake. Thus, where improvements are sought in financial management, the consultant will be asked to analyse existing arrangements, identify shortcomings and recommend improvements.

### Outputs

These will be the results of the various activities that the consultant will have to undertake in order to successfully complete the assignment. Depending on the project you may be in a position to specify the outputs before it starts or you may want the consultant to come forward with proposals for what these should be. In the financial management example above, the outputs might be a written report setting out recommendations for improvements and presentations to the board.

### Methodology

It can usually be left to the consultant to set out their proposed methodology for delivering the outputs. In the finance example above, the consultant might propose interviews with finance staff and senior managers, a review of financial reporting arrangements, an assessment of the existing accounting package and a review of alternative financial software.

### Management arrangements

How will the project be managed? Will it be by a steering group or a project manager? If it is by a steering group, who will decide on membership of the group and on what criteria will this be based? Which individual in the group is the consultant's principal point of contact with authority to agree changes to the brief, methodology or contract?

### Timescale

There is often a particular period during which the work needs to be undertaken for it to be of most, or even any, use. Where this is the case, start and finish dates need to be agreed and met.

### Budget

It is important to be clear from the outset about the amount of money available to employ a consultant. Setting out on a grandiose assignment is no use if there isn't going to be enough money. There is usually some scope for negotiating with consultants in order to try and conduct an assignment within the available resources, but that will take you only so far. If finance really is a problem then you might consider the alternatives outlined in Chapter 2 or, if there is time, it may be necessary to raise some funding before inviting expressions of interest.

## Presenting versus underlying problems

It may be that what you want done is quite straightforward and simply requires certain skills or assistance (for example, running a training course or launching a campaign). However, this isn't always the case and there may be times when there is something else that needs addressing first before the 'presenting' problem can be dealt with. For example, a request to devise a fundraising strategy may be the result of failures on the part of the fundraising staff and therefore the first task may really be to sort this out.

In these circumstances there are several scenarios:
- you identify the underlying problem as a result of going through the process of drawing up the initial brief
- the consultant brings it to your attention as the project progresses and the assignment has to be altered
- it is identified as a result of the consultancy and further action is required
- it is never resolved.

Be prepared for your consultant to want to discuss this with you at the outset

## Getting behind a 'presenting problem'

Our income was reducing due to lottery grants finishing and we decided that we needed to establish a trading arm to make money for the charity. We approached a funder and were fortunate enough to secure a grant to employ a consultant for five days in order to advise us.

His initial reaction was that we did not actually need any help with setting up a trading arm. Rather, he took us through a process of looking at our vision and mission statement. This led us to adopt a new vision statement which we are all very happy with. As well as the council of management a number of our team leaders were also involved, although there was a resistance to involve all of the staff team probably in the belief that the strategic aims needed to be agreed by the trustees.

As a result we were able to develop a three-year strategic plan with the consultant and this led to developing a business plan. In addition, the consultant helped us to look at our fundraising strategy and at the areas of fundraising that we could develop. Although the consultant's final report didn't meet the original objective of helping us to establish a trading arm, we felt that the whole experience had proved very positive for us as an organisation and had been a creative way of taking us forward.

It seemed that the consultant had not been sent a copy of our original application by the funder and therefore establishing a trading arm hadn't been properly understood as our starting point. Thus, establishing clear aims and objectives in relation to the consultant's role is something that needs to be done early. Nevertheless, we came out of the consultancy with a very exciting vision statement and strategic plan that has been welcomed by both staff and the council of management. In addition, now that we are clearer on the direction of the organisation we feel much better placed to assess how we might go about establishing trading activities, possibly without the help of a consultant.

**William Clemmey**
**Chief Executive, Warwickshire Association**
**Of Youth Clubs**
**www.wayc.org.uk**

## Commissioning consultants

I wish I'd known what I now know, when I was commissioning consultants: the benefit of hindsight is a wonderful thing. What follows is a selection of insights about what to expect and what's reasonable in your use of external consultants.

Much depends on the type of consultancy work you are commissioning. If it's a research or policy piece then expectations, roles and responsibilities are much more straightforward. You usually have a clear idea about the subject matter and the skills needed to undertake the work.

However, if the work is more developmental, or involves some strategic review or change process, you should be looking for a consultant who can add value to what you are doing, not to take over the work of internal staff. Don't expect your consultant to do it for you. A prospective client of mine once declared herself just 'too busy' to develop and write the organisation's business plan. Expect your consultant to ask lots of questions about how you see the issue at hand and to help you to get some clarity about it, not to just agree with you about how to solve the problem.

Consultancy in my book is more an art than a science. Having a consultant with lots of management experience and theories may be helpful, but how does he or she see the project developing? What's your consultant's preferred style of working? Is she or he coming in as an 'expert' or 'change leader', or more as an 'enabler' or 'facilitator'? More importantly, are you clear about the type of consultant you are looking for?

Give your project time to develop. 'Can you start next week and finish in two months?' is a common request. Most consultants, or at least the ones worth their salt, will be looking for new projects up to a month or so in advance. Projects take time to set up and get going, dates have to be booked in people's diaries well in advance and rushing the process, especially if it's a change process, just seems to harm it.

continued...

Once you have a clear idea about the working style, the appropriate role of the consultant and the timescales, get as clear as you can about your outcomes and what you expect to see at the end of the work. Many clients I work with find it hard to put their finger on what they actually want from the work, but time spent debating and defining clear achievable outcomes and clarifying all these points will pay enormous dividends later on.

**Linda Mitchell**
**Independent consultant**
**www.lindajoymitchell.org.uk**

## Developing an evolving brief

It started with a distinct feeling that there was a lot to learn. The Community Foundation Network (CFN) knew that the 55 community foundations in its network had lots of information at their fingertips about the powerful impact of their grant giving – but that they were not using it to promote their work to new donors.

When the consultant and CFN first met, we had an idea of where we wanted to arrive at, but didn't know how to get there. The 'dance' started with an agreement to work together for two months and then review progress. We encapsulated our thinking, as best we could, in a letter of understanding, but the main thing which bound us was a shared commitment to make it work, based on mutual trust.

Commitment and trust grew, as did confidence, in the steps we were taking. The second phase of the project – five months – was based on a clear written understanding and monthly retainer and involved facilitated meetings with five foundations who brought together groups of grant recipients.

We'd learnt a lot by working together and wanted others to join the dance. We captured the dance steps in an electronic how-to-do-it toolkit and sent round an invitation to all foundations to join us on the dance floor – to learn the steps, add their own and pilot the toolkit. This became the third phase of the project – six months.

continued...

In learning to dance together we've each had our own distinct moves to make and our own distinct roles to play. But over time, as we've learned each other's styles, and with generosity and trust, we have learned to dance as one for the benefit of community foundations and the brilliant work they do.

**Stephen Hammersley, Community Foundation Network**
**Martin Farrell, get2thepoint**
**Martin.farrell@get2thepoint.org.uk**

# 5 Finding and selecting the right consultant

This chapter sets out the options available for finding a consultant and how you should go about the selection process.

Should you use an existing contact or a new consultant?
- Finding someone new

Inviting expressions of interest
- Contact by telephone
- Invitation to submit a proposal
- What to send to prospective consultants

The selection process
- Shortlisting
- Setting up interviews
- The interview
- Taking up references
- Feedback communication with unsuccessful candidates

## Should you use an existing contact or a new consultant?

Time is always a scarce resource and lack of time often leads people to look for shortcuts. Sometimes these can work out well, but on other occasions they may end up causing additional, possibly costly, work.

When looking for a consultant there is an understandable temptation to turn to someone you already know or have used before. It may be that you have an existing relationship with a consultant who knows the organisation well and understands your business. If the consultant has the expertise you require and is not compromised in any way by previous work undertaken for you, then engaging him or her could be a good choice.

However, although the quality of the relationship with the consultant is vital, it is equally important to recruit someone with the right knowledge, experience and skills to undertake what needs to be done, so you may need to look elsewhere.

## The value of longer-term relationships with consultants

Organisations should be careful not to become complacent and simply slip into regularly using the same consultant, even where assignments are similar. However, finding a new consultant that suits your needs can be as difficult as finding the right candidate for a regular job. Thus, if you have a consultant who is capable, reliable and cost-effective there are a range of benefits that can arise out of developing a longer-term relationship:

- you know the consultant's track record and have confidence that she or he can deliver what you need
- your organisation can secure contracts that you can trust your consultant to deliver on your behalf
- regular exposure to your organisation gives a consultant insight into its culture, approach and the personalities involved
- fees for regular work can be negotiated
- easier access to an outside perspective you trust and respect
- regular contact with a consultant can lead to more opportunities to share knowledge and insight from experience gained elsewhere
- the benefits of good partnership that go beyond an often limited 'client–contractor' relationship
- insight into appropriate solutions when considering different options for your organisation
- you are more likely to be able to discuss work with the consultant before commissioning, to get feedback on what would be most useful and what would best meet the organisation's needs
- your organisation benefits from the consultant spending fewer desk days at the start of each project reading all the relevant documentation and meeting relevant personnel
- a quicker response, helpful when research findings are needed quickly in response to emerging policy issues
- you can build on the knowledge or insight from previous work in your organisation.

How do you know if your consultant is worth developing into a longer-term relationship? You'll want someone who is:
- accessible
- reliable
- cost-effective
- trustworthy
- capable of demonstrating mutual respect
- competent.

'A consultant we regularly use brings us skills and abilities that we can't afford on a full-time basis. However, we're able to offer those abilities to a third party with whom we have a contract which came to us because it trusts our brand and service. This arrangement raises our profile as a service provider, is valued by clients for its quality and usefulness, and is affordable because the work is fee-based and is flexible.'
Disability Charity

**Chris Avanti**
**Independent consultant**
**Chris.avanti@ukonline.co.uk**

### Finding someone new

There are various ways in which you can identify new consultants who might be able to undertake your assignment.

#### Colleagues/other organisations

Ask colleagues or people from other similar organisations for advice. Personal references are very important and you are likely to be able to pick up a lot of useful information quickly about a prospective consultant from another organisation.

However, to make sure that you find out what you really need, you should undertake the following when enquiring about a consultant:
- talk to the person in the organisation who actually dealt with the consultant in question
- establish what the consultant was actually asked to do and whether she or he completed the task successfully
- explore any similarities with the assignment you have in mind
- check on how well the organisation got on with the consultant – was he or she reliable, flexible and so on?
- ask about the consultant's fees and charges.

### Directories of consultants

Various organisations produce directories, either as hard copy or online (see Appendix 6), that provide extensive lists of consultants.

These can be very useful and provide access to consultants whom you might not be aware of. However, it's not always clear to what extent the compiler of the directory will have been able to screen entries prior to inclusion and what checks, if any, have been carried out on the consultants' performance. Therefore, it is often a case of 'buyer beware'.

If you identify a consultant who looks promising, find out as much as you can about him or her, for example, by using the consultant's website. You may also want to contact the consultant for a preliminary conversation to find out more.

### Advertisements/internet

Many consultants advertise and this is another avenue to explore. Trade magazines, professional journals and the internet are good places to start.

In most cases you will end up looking at consultants' websites. These will of course sing their praises. However, study them carefully to work out their specialty areas and to see which organisations they have worked for. Again, if they look promising get in touch for a preliminary chat.

### Universities

There is a large community of academics, especially from business schools, who may be well placed to help.

At some universities there may be dedicated consultancy services, while at others it may be a question of finding a suitably qualified academic who is in a position to undertake consultancy work.

## Inviting expressions of interest

Having identified some prospective consultants, the next step is to decide how best to approach them about your assignment. How you go about this is likely to be guided by the size and complexity of the task.

### Contact by telephone

As a first step you may want to start off by contacting prospective consultants by telephone in order to establish their availability and interest, and also to screen out those individuals or firms who appear to be unsuitable.

In the case of smaller assignments you may want to use this screening process to actually identify consultants who you will go on to interview, subject to their submitting a proposal.

### Invitation to submit a proposal

The next step is to send information about the assignment, along with details of what you require by way of a written proposal, to the consultants in which you are interested.

Where it's a substantial piece of work you may decide to adopt a two-stage approach. This involves a number of consultants being asked to submit a preliminary proposal involving only a limited amount of information. You can then use these to draw up a further shortlist of perhaps two or three who you ask to make a full proposal.

This approach may well yield better results because many consultants are understandably wary of committing significant resources with little expectation of success. Furthermore, experience suggests that those consultants who are willing to pitch for work with little idea of their chances of success are likely to perform less well.

There may be occasions when you decide to place an advertisement inviting tenders from interested consultants. This could be a requirement of a funder. While this has the advantage of possibly reaching consultants who might not otherwise have been known to you, it can be expensive, will take longer and may put off many potentially suitable consultants who haven't the resources to bid speculatively for contracts. Thought should be given to the most effective places to place advertisements, depending on the nature of the work and the kind of consultant you wish to attract.

### How many proposals to invite?

There are no hard and fast rules about this. For a very small job you may want to invite only one or two consultants to put themselves forward and you may only interview one. This could well be the case where you have conducted preliminary interviews over the telephone. More usually, submissions will be sought from between two and four consultants, with a view to interviewing two or three of them.

How you proceed and whether you go to tender will also be influenced by the urgency of the work and the resources available to handle the process.

### What to send to prospective consultants

How much information it is appropriate to send out will depend on the nature of the project, but it should include something in re-lation to each of the following items.

#### Information about your organisation

Your annual report and perhaps accounts are likely to suffice: the purpose is to provide details of the organisation's objectives and values, its size, structure and turnover. You should also include who prospective consultants can contact within your organisation for more information.

#### Objectives and the anticipated outputs

These will be drawn from the initial project brief (see Chapter 4) and you might ask the consultants to propose appropriate outputs. However, where the outputs have been identified clearly you may wish to be fairly prescriptive. For instance, if you want the consultant to produce a report, you could specify the format (hard copy or electronic), the number of copies and to whom it will go.

#### Qualities being sought in prospective consultants

You may want to include details of the sort of knowledge, experience and skills you believe are necessary to undertake the assignment. This will help prospective consultants to understand the organisation's expectations and assist them to decide whether to submit a proposal.

#### Timescale/deadline for submissions

This includes when you want the work to start and when you expect it to be completed, together with a deadline for written submissions of interest.

#### Budget

You need to choose whether or not to indicate the resources that you have available to finance the consultancy assignment. Revealing the price will enable the consultants to understand how much money is available and will prevent abortive bids, but you may prefer to leave it to the consultants to describe what they can do and how much it would cost in light of what you require.

#### What consultants should submit

You should provide clear instructions as to what you want prospective consultants to include in their proposal. The amount of detail you require will be determined by the complexity of the assignment. This will include:

- proposed methodology: their understanding of the task, how they would approach it and how they would propose to work with your organisation
- proposed timetable (including their availability)
- proposed costings, including an explanation of how their time is charged, whether VAT is chargeable and details of anticipated expenses, if these are likely to be a significant cost
- details of their firm/practice and of any similar work it has undertaken and if it was for similar organisations
- CVs of the person or persons who would be involved in undertaking the work, highlighting relevant experience, knowledge and skills
- details of two or three past clients who can be contacted for a reference once the consultants have submitted their proposals – it would be helpful if there were similarities between the work undertaken for the referees and the proposed assignment
- confirmation that they hold professional indemnity insurance
- details of any code(s) of practice to which they adhere in relation to quality or equal opportunities and so on.

## The selection process

This section sets out the steps you should take to select a consultant from the proposals you receive. However systematic you might be, in order to arrive at the right decision it will always require someone, or a group of people, to exercise their judgement. No set of procedures in themselves is going to tell you who you should take on.

## Selecting consultants

To begin with, write a good clear brief which spells out what you want the project to achieve.

For a major project, you may want to go through a two stage process: first identify people who are suitable and then shortlist for interview those who have given you a good proposal. Don't shortlist more than three or four consultants – they need to feel that they have a good chance of succeeding in order to make it worth their while to do a lot of work at risk, for which they won't be paid.

Make sure that the consultants you choose will be able to properly understand your organisation and your issues. If it's a complicated project, and it may change direction, then make sure that the consultants have the right set of skills and resources available to handle the revised project. Furthermore, if you're dealing with a firm of consultants, then ensure that they have identified a single point of contact who is able, if necessary, to redeploy resources as the project develops.

By the time the consultant completes the project you should make sure that your organisation has benefited practically and that they are leaving you with greater capacity and/or understanding and knowledge than you had before.

Finally, budget realistically – don't expect something for nothing.

**Greg Campbell**
**Campbell Tickell**
**www.campbelltickell.com**

### Shortlisting

In the case of some small projects you may have already screened prospective consultants via a telephone interview and sought only one or two submissions. You might decide then to interview only the most promising candidate. Where a number of consultants have been invited to make full submissions, the next step will be to select whom you wish to interview. If you've opted for a two-stage approach, then you'll need to decide how many of the respondents to invite to make a further submission.

In either case, you need to decide who will be involved in making the decision and on what basis. It could be done by one person, but depending on how many other members of staff are involved, you might want to involve some or all of them.

In comparing proposals and deciding which consultants to interview you should take the following into account:

- Outputs: Does the proposal properly address the assignment and describe what outputs the consultant would produce to meet it?
- Methodology: Is it well thought out and thorough?
- Empathy: Does the proposal demonstrate an understanding of your organisation and identify with its values, commitment and enthusiasm?
- Slippage: Does the proposal set out how the consultant proposes handling any slippage/overruns?
- Complaints: Does the proposal make clear how the consultant will deal with complaints about her or his own performance and actions to address this?
- Fees: The cheapest may not necessarily give you the best value. Look beyond the bottom line and bear in mind that a cheap quote may conceal hidden costs.
- Timescales and availability: Does the proposal demonstrate that the consultant is available for the times required, and that he or she will be able to fulfil the assignment within your timeframe?

Where there's uncertainty over aspects of a proposal don't hesitate to talk to the consultant in order to clarify things.

### Setting up interviews

How you approach interviewing consultants depends on a variety of factors. These include the number of consultants you've shortlisted, the timescale involved and the availability of other colleagues.

When issuing invitations to interviewees make it clear, especially to larger consultancies, that you wish to interview the people who will undertake the work so that you are able to make a judgement on the experience of those who are actually assigned to the project.

Before holding the interviews, clarify what charges or expenses the consultants may expect for simply attending. Normally you would reimburse their expenses for attending the interview but you would not pay for their time.

The panel

Who should conduct the interviews will depend on various considerations. In the case of projects concerned with the organisation's mission or governance, it is common for board members to be involved as well as staff. Where there is to be a steering committee then all or some of these might be involved. For smaller assignments it may be necessary for only one person to conduct the interviews.

**The interview**

Interviewing prospective consultants is not the same as conducting a recruitment interview: it is much more of a two-way process providing an opportunity for discussion and perhaps negotiation.

The interview needs to be well planned. If a presentation is required then you should have made this clear beforehand, together with arrangements for the presentation, for example, should the consultant bring their own laptop or overhead projector?

Interview questions

You should work out your questions in relation to the brief itself and to each consultant's proposals. The questions should explore the following areas:

- understanding of the assignment, the required outputs and the consultant's proposed methodology
- knowledge and experience of your sector – does the consultant understand the environment in which you operate? How much does she or he invest in developing/ maintaining knowledge of the sector?
- empathy with the values of your organisation
- interest in your work and willingness to learn about your organisation
- speciality areas or specific skills required to undertake the assignment
- similar work or projects the consultant may have undertaken in the past
- capacity and whether the consultant has the necessary resources available to complete the project on time
- ability to listen well
- rapport with your organisation and staff
- compensating factors that would make the consultant a good choice even if he or she is not familiar with your sector.

**Taking up references**

There may be a temptation to rely solely on your own judgement, especially if you feel you've found the 'right' person. However, a poor appointment could prove costly and therefore it's prudent to check with previous clients about past performance.

In some circumstances you may want to take up a verbal reference at the outset to help you to decide whether or not to interview someone. More frequently you will be taking up a reference having carried out an interview to confirm your decision or to help you decide between two competing consultants. In either case try to make sure that you're talking to someone who actually dealt with the consultant and knows his or her work at first hand. Some consultants may bring along or send in testimonies from previous clients; it's advisable to contact the people who have written these in order to verify what is said.

What to ask

Referees may be reluctant to volunteer information so you will need to ask a number of leading questions. The key points to explore are:
- Was the work carried out to their satisfaction?
- Did staff find the consultant communicative and flexible?
- Did the project finish on time and within budget?

**Feedback/communication with the unsuccessful candidates**

Apart from being polite, there are self-interested reasons for doing this. It's not unheard of for clients to have second thoughts or for a consultant to default at a very early stage. In one of these circumstances you could find yourself returning to one of the candidates you initially rejected and offering him or her the assignment.

# 6 Briefing the chosen consultant

Put your agreement in writing
Confirm the assignment and outputs
Identify lines of accountability and reporting arrangements
Agree the timescale
Agree milestones
Agree final report or publication
Set out terms and conditions
- Start and finish dates
- Fees/taxation/expenses/payment
- Resolving conflicts/disputes
- Termination of contract
- Confidentiality
- Conflicts of interest/restrictions
- Copyright/publication

It's important to get off to a good start and this means making sure that both parties are clear about what is expected from one another and what needs to be achieved. If there is confusion at the outset, then you are storing up problems for the future.

David Tyler, CEO of Community Matters, puts it like this: 'To ensure that you get what your organisation needs from your consultants make sure you are able to agree clear terms and conditions. It is OK to ask for help to devise what you need, but make sure everyone understands what has been decided in the end!'

## Put your agreement in writing

To achieve clarity you need to set out in writing how you wish the assignment to be undertaken and on what terms and conditions.

One approach is to include everything in one detailed contract that is drawn up specifically for the assignment. However, having to produce a contract for each piece of work could turn out to be a somewhat daunting task. There is a danger that the paperwork won't get done before the work is due to start which means it might not get done at all.

Another approach is to agree the brief for the particular assignment with the consultant and append it to what is basically a standard contract (see Appendix 2) or, if the assignment is relatively straightforward, a letter of appointment (see Appendix 3).

The brief will then focus on the assignment itself. The nature and complexity of the task will determine the level of detail, but it should cover the objectives and the outputs, what is expected of the consultant and how both parties will work together. Alongside this, the contract (or letter of appointment) will set out the terms and conditions on which the consultant is employed.

This approach also has the advantage of creating a discrete document (that is, the brief) that lends itself to wider circulation and use within the organisation. This is far better than a single contract that details everything. Appendix 1 sets out the remaining information in this section as a checklist for you to complete for each assignment.

## Confirm the assignment and outputs

The consultant should already have set out his or her understanding of the assignment and the required outputs in the submitted proposal. These now need to be finalised. If there have been any changes then this is the point at which to record them.

If there are significant changes the consultant may want to have more time, which might even affect the fee. While this is not ideal, it would be better to identify and resolve these issues at the outset rather than have them crop up later and lead to problems or even disputes.

## Identify lines of accountability and reporting arrangements

The relationship between you and your consultant will depend largely on the personalities of those involved, but you can influence this by being clear about how this relationship will be organised. Ensure that everyone knows who is ultimately accountable for the assignment and to whom the consultant reports (day-to-day reporting by the consultant to your organisation is best managed by one person). This accountability may reside in an individual, a specially convened steering group, the management team or even the board.

## Agree the timescale

The original timescale needs to be revisited at this point to establish whether the projected timescale as originally envisaged can be adhered to, or whether alterations to the start and finish dates are now necessary.

In addition, it would be prudent to consider the implications of an over-run on the projected timetable, from the point of view of both the consultant and the organisation. You could leave this to be dealt with by negotiation at the point at which the problem arises, but there may be circumstances in which completion by the deadline is essential and it may even be appropriate to put in place penalties for late delivery.

## Agree milestones

It is good practice to identify a series of targets or milestones that need to be reached by an agreed time in order to make sure that the assignment proceeds successfully towards completion.

This usually means breaking up the project into stages, setting tasks that must be achieved within each stage and monitoring progress. Not only is this a good discipline for the client, it also helps to ensure that the consultant is being both systematic and realistic from the outset.

As part of this process it is advisable to:
- build in some slack to allow for unforeseen delays on either side, while not giving the impression that all your deadlines are negotiable

- build in opportunities for mutually agreeing amendments to the brief, though these may involve added expense if they require the consultant to commit extra resources.

## Agree final report or publication

If the consultancy is going to lead to a final report or publication, then a number of things need to be agreed. These include:
- the format in which the report will be presented
- the number of copies required
- a list of who you want to receive the report (though it may be simpler for your organisation to handle the actual distribution)
- whether the consultant will be required to make a presentation and if so at which meeting(s)
- what role, if any, the consultant will have in implementing the recommendations. This should be carefully considered before any decision is taken. Apart from the question of resources, you need to decide whether or not to continue with the same consultant (see Chapter 8).

## Set out terms and conditions

### Start and finish dates
Given that preliminary discussions and possibly even meetings are likely to take place, it's important that both parties are clear about when the assignment actually commences and from which point the consultant can start charging for her or his time.

The contract should specify the actual date on which the assignment begins and either the finish date or the number of days/hours for which the consultant has been engaged.

### Fees/taxation/expenses/payment
This is also the time to confirm in writing the basis on which the consultant will be paid. There are a number of different aspects to address, depending on the assignment.

#### Fees
If it has been agreed that the consultant will be paid a fixed fee on the successful delivery of the outputs, then this is the figure that should appear. If the fixed price relates to a specific number of days, then it would also be advisable to specify in writing the rate at which any further days would be charged if the contract ends up being extended.

If the consultant is being paid by the day/hour, this amount needs to be specified, possibly along with a maximum number of days that can be claimed or the point (number of days) at which she or he must refer back to the client.

If more than one consultant is involved, and different consultants are paid at different rates, this needs to be made clear.

If it is likely that work may have to be undertaken at weekends or in the evenings, then it needs to be made clear whether or not this will be charged at a higher rate.

You should also establish how peripheral extras such as travel and preparation time will be treated.

### Taxation

It should be made clear that the consultant is responsible for paying his or her own tax. Also, establish if VAT will be on top of the fee. You don't want to find that 17.5 per cent has unexpectedly been added to the bill.

### Expenses

Specify the procedures for authorising and claiming expenses and the documentation you will require (that is, receipts). Discuss what expenses are included in the fee and what are not – for instance, telephone calls, postage, travel and so on.

Specify delegated authority to purchase anything on behalf of the organisation if this is likely to arise (for example, an IT consultant may need to purchase certain pieces of equipment).

### Payment

You might opt for phased/staged payments or payment on completion. It might also be appropriate to give an undertaking as to the time that will be needed to process invoices, though it may be difficult to do this if these are processed by another department.

You may also want to specify penalties for late delivery or non-performance.

Finally, there might be circumstances in which it is appropriate to negotiate a retention, payable at some agreed point after the assignment has been completed – for example, when the consultant has installed a new IT system or accounting package.

### Resolving conflicts/disputes

A clause needs to be included setting out arrangements for resolving any disputes that cannot be settled by negotiation. For example, this could arise where the organisation refuses to pay the consultant on account of poor performance and no compromise can be reached.

The most common approach, which avoids recourse to the courts, is to agree to refer the matter to an arbitration service whose decision will be binding on both parties. NCVO runs a scheme in conjunction with the Centre For Dispute Resolution and this could be included in the contract.

### Termination of contract

There are two eventualities in relation to termination of the contract.

Provision needs to be made for either party to give notice to the other that they wish to withdraw from the assignment. The amount of notice required will relate to the nature of the assignment and how long it would take to arrange an orderly withdrawal or handover. This would normally be a matter of weeks, but in the case of a complicated IT assignment an extended period might be necessary.

The other circumstance is where there is breach of contract on either side or a case of gross misconduct (for example, breach of confidence) – in these circumstances termination can be immediate.

### Confidentiality

The contract needs to state that the consultant is prohibited from divulging to third parties anything that is confidential to the client without the client's explicit permission.

### Conflicts of interest/restrictions

There also needs to be a clause that prevents the consultant working for one or more of the organisation's competitors during the assignment without the organisation's consent.

### Copyright/publication

Where there is a publication involved there will need to be conditions laid down relating to:

- amendments to the final draft
- disclosure by the consultant to third parties
- the organisation's ownership of and access to the research
- the organisation holding the copyright to the publication.

# 7 Managing the relationship

This chapter looks at how to manage the contractual relationship with the consultant.

Brief other staff in the organisation
Organise an induction for the consultant
Ensure availability of staff time and resources
Facilitate dialogue between the organisation and the consultant
Monitor progress and the timetable
Manage the budget
Deal with disputes

Good relationships with consultants ultimately depend on the people involved possessing the necessary personal skills and judgement to make them work. As Robina Rafferty, CEO of Housing Justice, says, 'The chemistry of your relationship with the consultant is really important. You need someone who is on the same wavelength and with whom you can always have a frank and honest debate.'

Nevertheless, there are variety of factors which, even if they can't guarantee good working relations, do underpin them. The following sections examine what these are.

## Brief other staff in the organisation

Make sure that everyone who needs to know is aware of the assignment, who has been appointed to it and when it starts. This sounds like commonsense, but it's amazing how things like this can be overlooked and how quickly rumours start.

You should try to achieve a high level of ownership among those actually commissioning the consultant (for example, the management team) and buy-in among the staff affected by the consultant's work.

However, there will be circumstances in which this will be difficult to achieve – for example, if the assignment is about something like reorganisation, which may be perceived as potentially threatening some people's jobs.

## Organise an induction for the consultant

Depending on the scale of the project it might be appropriate to provide an induction pack for the consultant and/or a short induction programme involving meetings with key members of staff and perhaps trustees.

At this point it will also be appropriate to clarify with the consultant what, if any, delegated authority she or he is being assigned. For instance, if the consultant is being asked to conduct an assignment connected to IT, then it may be appropriate for this individual to have authority to alter certain functions relating to the IT system. At the same time, it should be made clear to staff what delegated authority has been granted and when it can be exercised.

## Ensure availability of staff time and resources

On occasion the consultant will need access to various members of staff, possibly board members and sometimes the organisation's resources.

Accordingly, plan ahead and make sure that:
- the staff who are involved with the assignment have or are given the necessary time and resources to work with the consultant
- arrangements are made for the consultant to have access to your board and clients if necessary
- the consultant has use of the organisation's facilities and access to any necessary information and data in order to complete the work.

## Facilitate dialogue between the organisation and the consultant

There needs to be someone who is ultimately responsible for the consultant's work and to whom he or she reports. Failure to establish clear and unambiguous lines of communication is often one of the factors that leads to problems arising between consultants and their clients.

For bigger projects there may be a steering group, but it still needs to be clear who is the project leader and who within the steering group has the ultimate responsibility.

If appropriate, arrangements should be made for regular feedback from the consultant to other staff as the assignment progresses.

## Monitor progress and the timetable

The milestones that were agreed at the outset should provide the basis for jointly reviewing progress against the final outputs and the timetable. These reviews can be used in a number of ways:
- as an opportunity for amending or revising the brief, which may mean an adjustment to the consultant's fees
- as an opportunity to identify and resolve any problems that may have arisen on either side
- as an opportunity to tackle poor performance on the part of the consultant.

If the consultant identifies unforeseen problems or issues that need to be tackled before the main assignment can be undertaken, or which simply also need to be addressed in their own right, then it may be necessary to amend the brief for the whole assignment. For example, a consultant engaged to undertake a job evaluation might discover that job descriptions are inadequate and need to be reviewed and rewritten.

---

### Dealing with poor performance

You may find yourself dealing with a poorly performing consultant and come up against problems such as:
- missed deadlines
- poor relations with project staff
- disagreements over the interpretation of the brief
- communication difficulties – unreturned calls or emails
- poor quality of work.

Don't wait and hope things will improve. Convene a meeting as soon as possible to get things out in the open. Obtain the views of other colleagues and explain your concerns to the consultant. Refer back to the contract and the brief in order to substantiate your concerns.

Aim to arrive at a consensus as to the nature of the problems that have arisen and to agree how they can be resolved:
- set deadlines for improved performance and subsequent reviews
- set out these conclusions in writing and give this to the consultant.

**continued...**

---

If the problems persist then reconvene the discussion with the consultant or, if appropriate, consider referring the matter to a more senior individual, if this is an option.

Alternatively, it may be that a better course of action is to terminate the contract by giving the agreed period of notice (or immediately if there are material grounds for breach of contract).

Faced with poor performance, don't prevaricate; it is better to confront the problem and try and resolve it rather than hope things will improve and then find it's too late to take action.

## Manage the budget

It is essential to keep control of expenditure and manage the budget carefully, especially if it's a large project.

At the point at which the consultant was commissioned, details of all fees and expenses should have been clarified. This includes procedures for payment (see Chapter 6).

Before the consultant starts work make sure that:

- a procedure is in place for authorising all invoices submitted by the consultant – these should be authorised by the project manager who will be in a position to know whether the work has been carried out properly and/or expenses incurred
- systems exist that will enable you to get up-to-date and accurate information about expenditure and the relevant staff are aware of these procedures
- any invoices that have been submitted for work that either hasn't been completed or is unsatisfactory are discussed with the consultant.

If it appears that the assignment is in danger of going over budget then you should discuss this immediately with the consultant to establish why this is the case and what can be done to retrieve the situation.

## Deal with disputes

The procedure for dealing with disputes should be set out in the contract, but it is always best to try to resolve disagreements amicably before resorting to formal procedures.

You should meet up with the consultant in order to try to reach an agreement or compromise. This could be in relation to a whole range of things such as a disagreement about the interpretation of the brief, a breakdown in personal relations at some level or a disagreement concerning payment. Unless the consultant's performance is unsatisfactory and/or personal relations have broken down irretrievably, it is usually bestaim for some sort of compromise in order to save the assignment.

If the situation cannot be resolved by the two parties and terminating the consultancy is not an option, then it may be necessary to seek help from independent mediators (see Chapter 6).

---

### Managing consultant/client relationship

Keeping a good dialogue going during the project is really important – developments in the client organisation or in the outside world may affect the work you are doing and you need to be able to rely on the client to keep you informed of anything that might be significant, for example, staff changes or other changes in their plans. But, while a good consultant will be able to respond appropriately to changing circumstances, changing the actual brief or purpose of the consultancy on a frequent or ad hoc basis during the project can create problems for both parties. Frequent changes may be a sign of a bigger uncertainty that needs to be addressed, and a good consultant will be proactive about raising such issues.

In my experience it's always a good idea to probe a bit. The problem, as set out by the client, is not always the most significant one and you need to have a good dialogue at the outset in order to make sure you don't discover this too late. For example, an organisation may request 'help with fundraising' but when you start to work with it you discover that the reason it is struggling is that it lacks a clear mission and/or strategy and this is why it is finding it difficult to persuade funders.

continued...

---

There needs to be a clear timetable agreed with the client at the outset to manage everybody's expectations and avoid disputes. This is particularly important when the audience for the work is a board or advisory group rather than an individual. The client should inform the consultant of any key dates that are relevant for the project, for example, trustee meetings. Check deadlines for papers as these often need to go out at least a week in advance.

It's also a good idea at the outset to schedule in progress meetings at key points in the project to make sure everything stays on track. If things are left unchecked with the client, disputes are more likely to arise at the end of the project.

Finally, keep the emphasis on work – doing business informally over lunch may work for some people, but I'd rather keep the main part of the business formal and focused. Most consultants need to have quite a structured approach and take notes – which is difficult to do over a dining table (especially if you are actually hungry!). Once the main part of the business is done you can still have a chat over lunch and talk more freely, perhaps focusing on any grey areas remaining. I have found this approach is more likely to bring useful insights to the work and to keep costs down for the client.

**Jean Barclay**
**Freelance consultant**
**jeanbarclay@velvetevolution.com**

# 8 Implementing recommendations and evaluating the consultancy

This chapter looks at how to agree final outputs, manage and implement the recommendations, and evaluate both the outcomes and the consultancy.

Getting recommendations agreed
- What to do if you disagree with the recommendations

Handling the consequences of recommendations carefully

Acting on the recommendations
- Logistical considerations
- Financial considerations

A further role for the consultant?

Evaluating the consultancy
- Were the consultancy objectives met?

Did the consultancy contribute to bringing about the desired change?

All management consultancy assignments should result in some material changes to the way in which an organisation is run. Hopefully these will reflect closely the outcomes that the consultant's work was intended to bring about.

Some consultancy assignments, involving for example training or mentoring, actually deliver the desired outcome by changing the way people behave or their performance. Others result in a set of recommendations that then have to be implemented in order to bring about the desired changes (for example, where the assignment is about reorganisation or purchasing IT equipment).

## Getting recommendations agreed

If there has been a regular dialogue between both parties then it's unlikely that the recommendations will contain any shocks. Nevertheless, it often makes sense to ask the consultant for a draft report that can be discussed with colleagues and possibly board members.

This will help to ensure that the final report deals with what you asked for and as far as possible meets your needs. If this is not the case, it's possible that there may be fundamental disagreements that cannot easily be resolved. However, in most circumstances it should be possible to negotiate changes or additions.

If there are confidential issues dealt with in the final report then they may need to be set out in a separate document/annex addressed to the chief executive and/or the board.

### What to do if you disagree with the recommendations

This is a difficult area because some consultants will take the view that it is their job to draw the conclusions or make the recommendations that they believe to be correct. However, it's also important that their findings can be used to improve the organisation. Accordingly, there may be occasions when it's quite reasonable for negotiations to take place in order to ensure that recommendations are what Greg Campbell, from Campbell Tickell Associates, calls 'realistic and deliverable', especially in terms of what is logistically or financially possible.

If this situation is likely to arise then it's best to raise the problem as soon as possible in advance of the final report being submitted to allow scope for negotiation with the consultant.

Nevertheless, there may be other situations in which consultants believe they have no alternative other than to make recommendations that will be unwelcome for some parties, such as criticism or condemnation of senior management or specific individuals. In these circumstances it may be necessary to seek further external assistance to decide how best to deal with what may be very sensitive issues.

## Handling the consequences of recommendations carefully

Sometimes a consultant's recommendations may pose problems for certain people within the organisation and therefore it is important to carefully manage the process by which they are made public.

Also, since recommendations are not always accepted in the form in which they are initially presented, and sometimes not at all, it's important to keep them confidential until final decisions have been made. Failure to do this may result in misinformation and staff reacting adversely to anticipated changes that may never actually occur. Situations of this nature can be damaging and, at the very least, are likely to take valuable time and energy to resolve.

Given this, think carefully about to whom and when the recommendations will be made available. It may be important that some people receive them before others; for instance, usually managers will need to know in advance of their staff.

The biggest problem is making time to ensure that arrangements are in place to prevent things going wrong, rather than a lack of understanding about what's at stake.

## Acting on the recommendations

Having received the consultant's recommendations the next step is to decide what action should be taken. This may be a logistical matter, a financial matter or both.

### Logistical considerations

Make sure that a proper plan is drawn up around implementation and that those affected by what is being proposed are consulted and involved appropriately. Also, make sure that affected staff have the time and resources to deal with any extra work that is created. For example, the recommendations could be about increasing membership, which would be likely to generate additional work.

### Financial considerations

If the consultant's recommendations require additional expenditure, for instance on training, new staff, or equipment, then the organisation will need to find this extra spending. Ideally it will have been possible, at the outset, to earmark some money to implement recommendations, but where this is not the case the consultant's report and recommendations could form the basis of a proposal for funding.

## A further role for the consultant?

It may be that the consultant has a role to play in assisting with implementing the recommendations. Obviously this will depend on the knowledge and experience that is necessary and who is required to undertake the work.

However, where the existing consultant meets the person specification and has performed well, consideration should be given to retaining him or her. The consultant's understanding of your organisation and the relationships that he or she may have established with members of staff should mean that retaining the consultant is a cost-effective solution.

## Evaluating the consultancy

There are two levels on which the success of a consultancy needs to be judged. The first is its success in achieving the objectives that were set (for instance, appraising a proposal to merge with another organisation). The second is in terms of the contribution that this makes to achieving the outcomes that drove the decision to commission a consultant (such as the need to make the organisation financially sustainable).

### Were the consultancy objectives met?

The first level can be assessed by judging how well the consultant carried out the work and how well she or he worked with the organisation and its staff.

With regard to the former, you should evaluate the following factors:

- Timetable: Was this adhered to and if it was necessary to amend it, was this negotiated in a satisfactory manner?
- Budget: Was the assignment delivered within budget? If there were variations, were these well handled?
- Outputs: Did the outputs that the consultant delivered (for instance, a training course or a report) result in the outcomes of the consultancy being met (staff being better able to do their jobs, proposals being put forward for reorganisation and so on)? Was your organisation satisfied with the quality of the outcomes and the way in which they were delivered (for example, presentation skills, written material, facilitation)?

With regard to how well the consultant generally worked with the organisation, there are a number of matters to take into account:

- Understanding of the business: Did the consultant properly understand the organisation's business?
- Empathy: Did people feel that the consultant was able to empathise with them and understand the challenges they faced?
- Communication: Did the consultant communicate well with members of staff and put people at their ease?
- Confidence: Did people generally feel confident in the consultant's ability to undertake the assignment?
- Chemistry: Was there generally a perception that the chemistry between the consultant and the organisation was good?
- Added value: Did staff feel that the consultant brought 'added value' to the organisation?

Taken together, this information should be used to:

- identify any mistakes that have been made, with a view to avoiding them in the future
- determine whether you employ the consultant again and how best to deploy him or her.

## Did the consultancy contribute to bringing about the desired change?

To judge what has been achieved at this second level entails taking a step back and looking at whether or not the consultancy has contributed towards, or brought about, the desired outcome for the organisation. For instance, did the appraisal pave the way for a merger and financial stability or not?

At this level the main concern is whether or not the assignment itself was correctly or incorrectly conceived. If it turns out that it was misconceived, then the lesson to be learned is that, regardless of whether or not the consultant does a good job, it needs to be the right job!

## Dealing with recommendations

The recommendations of any consultant should not be taken blindly. Many of the same considerations should be applied as one would use to vet a potential programme or project.

First, carefully review what is to be achieved. Second, assess resources required in terms of time, people, and cost of implementation. Third, conduct a benefit and beneficiary analysis to ensure that you are getting good value for money. Fourth, assess the cultural fit of the recommendations and their alignment with your mission and vision.

**Cynthia Hansen,**
**Director of Management Consultancy,**
**Action Planning**
**www.actionplanning.co.uk**

# Appendix 1:
# Consultancy checklist

**Do you need a consultant?**

1. What needs to be done?

2. Is an external consultancy needed and will it work?

**Working out what a consultant will do**

3. How will a consultant be used?

4. Setting out the task ahead of an appointment

**Making an appointment**

5. Finding and appointing a consultant

6. Briefing the chosen consultant

7. Managing the relationship

8. Dealing with recommendations and evaluating the consultancy

**Contract checklist**

9. Drawing up a contract with a consultant

## 1. What needs to be done?

| | |
|---|---|
| **1.1 Presenting issues**<br>What is the opportunity or problem that faces your organisation? | |
| **1.2 Evidence**<br>What evidence is there that suggests or confirms the need for some kind of action? | |
| **1.3 Ownership**<br>Is this analysis shared by those responsible for deciding to take action? | |
| **1.4 Timing**<br>By when does the opportunity or problem need to be addressed? | |
| **1.5 Consequence of taking no action**<br>What will happen if no action is taken? | |
| **1.6 Desired outcomes**<br>What changes need to take place?<br><br>What will 'success' look like?<br><br>How will the organisation be different? | |

## 2. Is an external consultancy needed and will it work?

| | |
|---|---|
| **2.1 Why use an external consultant?**<br>A lack of in-house knowledge?<br>A need for a new perspective and new insights? | |

| | |
|---|---|
| A need for a neutral and independent view?<br>A lack of capacity?<br><br>*See Chapter 1* | |
| **2.2 Are there other options?**<br>An in-house resource (staff or committee)<br>Pro bono assistance<br>A secondee<br>An interim appointment<br><br>If one or more of these is a possibility, then do the pros outweigh the cons?<br><br>*See Chapter 2* | |
| **2.3 Is there commitment within the organisation to a consultancy?**<br>Is there sufficient commitment within the organisation to support the work and make use of the outputs?<br><br>Is there commitment at an appropriately senior level in the organisation? | |
| **2.4 Are the resources available to support a consultant?**<br>Has the organisation staff available to work with a consultant?<br><br>Can they dedicate the necessary time?<br><br>*See Chapter 7* | |

| 3. How will a consultant be used? | |
|---|---|
| **3.1 How will you use the consultant?**<br>What sort of intervention do you require?<br><br>Analysis/strategy<br>Analysis leading to recommendations<br><br>Process management<br>Support for implementation<br><br>Enabler<br>Facilitation<br>Mediation<br><br>Passing on knowledge<br>Trainer<br>Mentor<br>Coach<br><br>*See Chapter 1* | |
| **3.2 What expertise is required from the consultant?**<br>What competencies (knowledge, experience and skills) will be needed by the consultant to undertake the task?<br><br>*See Chapters 1 and 4* | |

| 4. Setting out the task ahead of an appointment | |
|---|---|
| *See Chapter 4*<br><br>**4.1 Purpose of consultancy**<br>What are the agreed desired changes (outcomes) within the organisation or ways of working that need to happen? | |

| | |
|---|---|
| **4.2 The assignment/outputs**<br>What is the task that the consultant is being asked to undertake and what are the specific outputs that the consultant must produce to achieve this (for example, a report with recommendations/costings/timetable)? | |
| **4.3 Management of the consultant**<br>Who will commission the consultant and to whom will they report on a day-to-day basis? | |
| **4.4 Timescale**<br>Deadline for submission of tenders and decisions regarding appointment of consultant<br><br>Start and finish dates | |
| **4.5 Budget**<br>Financial parameters to the consultancy | |
| **5. Finding and appointing a consultant** | |
| **5.1 Finding a consultant**<br>What options are there?<br><br>Existing or new person?<br><br>Where to look?<br><br>*See Chapters 3 and 5* | |

**5.2 Inviting tenders**
What is an appropriate
tendering process for the
project?

How should consultants be
asked to respond to the brief?

Response to include:
- consultant's understanding
  of brief
- how they would approach
  the task (their methodology)
- proposed timetable
-  who would do the work
- CVs
- insurances
- costs/payment
  arrangements
- references

*See Chapter 5*

**5.3 Selection and
interviewing consultants**

How should you go about
shortlisting consultants?

How should you go about
interviewing prospective
consultants?

Who should conduct the
interview?

What should they be asked?

*See Chapter 5*

## 6. Briefing the chosen consultant

*See Chapter 6*

| | |
|---|---|
| **6.1 Confirm the assignment and outputs:**<br><br>Confirm what exactly the consultant will undertake/produce and how they will go about it (methodology) | |
| **6.2 Accountability and reporting arrangements**<br><br>What will be the arrangements for briefing the consultant at the outset and who will do it?<br><br>To whom will the consultant be accountable?<br><br>What will be the arrangements for the consultant to report back on progress/problems? (for example, frequency, meetings/phone)? | |
| **6.3 Timescale**<br><br>Agree the exact timescale (including start and completion dates) | |
| **6.4 Milestones**<br><br>Agree the stages at which you want to review rogress/receive any interim reports | |

| | |
|---|---|
| **6.5 Agree final report/presentation**<br><br>Confirm how the final outputs are to be submitted (for example, are reports to be simply submitted in writing or should the consultant be required to present them in person and also make a presentation?) | |
| **6.6 Resolving conflicts**<br><br>What arrangements need to be put in place for resolving conflicts that may arise?<br><br>Who within the organisation will have the final say? | |
| **6.7 Terminating the contract**<br><br>What arrangements need to be in place to enable either party to terminate the contract?<br><br>*NB: Other contractual items are set out in Section 9 below* | |
| **7. Managing the relationship** | |
| *See Chapter 7*<br><br>**7.1 Briefing other staff/the organisation**<br><br>Brief relevant members of staff about the consultancy | |
| **7.2 Induction for the consultant**<br><br>Ensure the consultant is properly inducted | |

| | |
|---|---|
| **7.3 Staff time resources**<br><br>Ensure that adequate staff time and resources are available to support the consultant | |
| **7.4 Dialogue between consultant and the organisation**<br><br>Depending on the size of the assignment, arrangements may need to be put in place to manage this | |
| **7.5 Monitoring progress and the timetable**<br><br>Use agreed milestones/reviews to monitor progress | |
| **7.6 The budget**<br><br>Costs need to be carefully managed against the original budget and any necessary amendments that arise during the assignment | |
| **7.7 Disputes/poor performance**<br><br>Disputes and poor performance need to be dealt with immediately in order to forestall further problems | |

## 8. Dealing with recommendations and evaluating the consultancy

*See Chapter 8*

| | |
|---|---|
| **8.1 Agreeing recommendations**<br><br>Hold discussions with the consultant around draft recommendations prior to production of the final report | |
| **8.2 Managing news of recommendations**<br><br>Put in place arrangements for dealing with news of recommendations within the organisation | |
| **8.3. Dealing with recommendations**<br><br>Do any steps need to be taken in advance to ensure that the necessary resources are available to deal with implementing recommendations that are accepted?<br><br>This might be the case in relation to either logistical or financial considerations | |
| **8.4 Evaluation**<br><br>What arrangements need to be made to ensure that an evaluation of the consultancy exercise is carried out?<br><br>The consultancy will need to be evaluated in terms of the | |

success in meeting the objectives set out for the consultant and also in terms of its success in bringing about the desired outcomes for the organisation

## 9. Drawing up a contract with a consultant

A contract sets out terms and conditions and should include:
- details of parties to the contract
- details of the proposed timescale (for example, commencement and completion)
- grounds and arrangements for termination on either side
- details of fees and expenses agreed in advance
- arrangements for invoicing and payment
- details as to how taxation will be dealt with
- requirements relating to confidentiality
- arrangements for dealing with disputes and mediation
- details of rights to intellectual ownership and publication
- requirements relating to avoiding conflicts of interest

The project brief may be appended since this sets out the scope of the work, accountabilities, outputs and deadlines

*See Appendix 2 for sample contract*

# Appendix 2:
# Sample contract for services or consultancy

**1. Introduction and Definitions:**

This Agreement is between _____ (organ-
isation's name and address) (herein after called 'the client') and
(_____ ) (herein after called 'the Consultant').

The Agreement will be in accordance with the following Terms
and Conditions unless and until an alternative is specifically
agreed between the Parties.

**2. Purpose of the Agreement:**

The purpose of the Agreement is:

_____

Further details of the Agreement are set out in the attached
Schedule*

> * The Schedule can take the form of the Brief to which the Consultant
> will be working. This can include:
> - the objectives & outputs
> - reporting arrangements and lines of accountability
> - milestones and related outputs
> - the detailed timetable.

**3. Commencement date and duration of the Agreement:**

This Agreement will commence on _____.
and will remain in effect until _____ or until the completion of the consultancy (delete as appropriate).

### 4. Termination:

The Agreement may be terminated by either party giving one month's notice in writing.

The Client may terminate the Agreement immediately in the event that the Consultant commits any material breach of the terms of this Agreement, or is guilty of gross misconduct.

### 5. Fees and expenses:

Fees for the Agreement will be as follows _____
(specify: hourly/daily rate + maximum hours/days or fixed price)

VAT will be added at the appropriate rate. (delete if VAT is not charged)

Appropriate, travel, subsistence and other expenses will be paid at cost, subject to evidence of expenditure and in accordance with arrangements specifically agreed in advance with the Consultant.

### 6. Invoices and payment:

Unless specifically agreed otherwise, invoices will be submitted monthly by the Consultant and payment made within 30 days.

### 7. Taxation:

The Consultant is a self-employed person responsible for taxation and National Insurance or similar liabilities or contributions in respect of the fees and the Consultant will indemnify the Client against all liability for the same and any costs, claims or expenses including interest and penalties.

### 8. Professional indemnity:

The Consultant is required to have professional indemnity insurance.

### 9. Confidentiality/Intellectual Ownership:

The Consultant will not divulge to third parties matters confidential to the client (whether or not covered by this Agreement) without the client's explicit permission.

Except where specifically agreed otherwise, all material, data, information etc. collected during the course of the Agreement will remain in the possession of the Client and not used without their permission.

**10. Publication of material:**

Where the Agreement provides for the publication of material, the following specific conditions shall apply:
(a)  The Client will retain the right to edit the final draft prior to publication subject, in the case of joint publications, to amendments proposed being agreed with the author(s).
(b)  Prior to publication, the Consultant and/or others associated with the publication shall not disclose any material obtained or produced for the purposes of the project to any other party unless the Client has given prior approval in writing.
(c)  The Consultant will provide to the client copies of all material, data etc. collected specifically for the project and indicate the source of other material used.
(d)  The Client will, except where specifically agreed otherwise, hold copyright to the publication.

Other matters relating to the use of the material shall be covered as an Appendix to this Agreement. Where other uses are agreed, all material and publications based on the project shall acknowledge _____ .

**11. Restrictions/Conflicts of interest:**

The Consultant shall not, whilst this Agreement is in force, be engaged or concerned directly or indirectly in the provision of services to any other party in the same or similar field of business or activity to _____ without the prior written consent of _____ .

**12. Disputes:**

In the event of a dispute that cannot be resolved by nego-tiation between the client and the consultant, the matter shall be referred to an arbitrator agreed by both parties. The decision of the arbitrator shall be final.
(This could be NCVO's own scheme run in conjunction with the Centre For Dispute Resolution.)

**13. Other conditions:**

Any other conditions, including variations to the terms set out above, shall be included as an Appendix to this Agreement.

For the Client _____ (Organisation)
Signed: _____
Date: _____
Name: _____
Designation: _____

For the Consultant
Signed: _____
Date: _____
Name: _____
Designation: _____

# Appendix 3:
# Sample letter of appointment (suitable for small assignments)

When a full contract is not appropriate as the job or the timescales or the organisation's resources or relationship with the provider do not warrant it, a Letter of Appointment may suffice. A sample letter is set out below.

Dear

Re: [enter project name]

I am pleased to accept your proposal dated DD/MM/YY.

Our project manager for this project will be [insert name]. We understand that your lead consultant will be [insert name].

The assignment will proceed on the following basis:

- key outputs: (detail these)
- timescale/milestones: (detail these)
- reporting arrangements: (detail these)
- confidentiality/termination arrangements: (detail these)

As agreed, the cost of the project will be [insert figure] expenses and VAT (if applicable). We ask that you invoice us as follows (e.g. 50% on commissioning and 50% on delivery of final report).

Please reply by [insert date] to confirm your acceptance of the assignment and these conditions.

Yours sincerely

[insert name]

# Appendix 4: Sample brief

## Background

Why XYZ organisation has decided to seek the services of a consultant, that is, interim support, additional capacity, skills not available within the organisation.

The outcomes that XYZ organisation is seeking to achieve are as follows:

[Insert – for example, to improve customer service within the organisation.]

## The assignment

Describe what the assignment entails, for example, to identify best practice, to assess training needs among staff or to deliver training.

There are X identified outputs/activities (relevant to this proposal). These are:

[List outputs and required activities as appropriate – for example, research other organisations, carry out a training needs analysis and design and deliver a training programme.]

## The consultant

XYZ organisation wishes to appoint a consultant to carry out the above assignment.

[List any desirable/essential requirements relating to knowledge/skills/experience that the consultant will need to possess to undertake the work.]

## Support/management

XYZ organisation will provide:

[Outline what information/support will be provided (if necessary).]

[Outline who will manage the relationship.]

## Timetable and costs

XYZ organisation requires the assignment to commence by ...............and to be completed by ....................

Submissions will need to come within the available budget, which is £....... (including VAT).

## Quality issues

XYZ organisation expects its contractors to embrace the following set of values and quality standards:

- a commitment to non-discriminatory practice and to ensuring equal opportunity in its work and interactions

- a respect for confidentiality

- a commitment to all text being produced in plain English and all recommendations being set out clearly.

## Contact details

Lead contact at XYZ organisation:

Telephone:

Address:

Deadline for submissions:

# Appendix 5:
# Sample reference request

**Date:**

**Name of consultant:**

**Organisation (if applicable):**

We are considering engaging the above consultant who has given your name as a referee. We would be very grateful if you could provide us with an assessment of their performance and brief details of the assignment with which they were involved. If you also feel able to add any comments, then this would be most helpful.

**The assignment (brief description/date):**

**1. Capability**

Evaluation:      1: n    2: n    3: n    4: n
(1 = high through to 4 = low)

Comments [for example: Did you receive a high-quality service? Did their level of expertise meet your expectations? Would you use them again and would you recommend them to others?]

**2. Delivery**

Evaluation:      1: n    2: n    3: n    4: n
(1 = high through to 4 = low)

Comments [for example: Did you discuss/receive a project plan and timetable ? Were you kept up to date with progress of the project? Was the project completed on time?]

### 3. Interpersonal relations

Evaluation:    1: ▢    2: ▢    3: ▢    4: ▢
(1 = high through to 4 = low)

Comments [for example: Were relations between yourself and the consultant satisfactory? Did the consultant relate well to staff members?]

Many thanks.

Name:

Position/organisation:

Please return to _____ by _____ .

# Appendix 6:
# Useful resources

## 1. Organisations maintaining a directory/listing of consultants

These organisations provide listings of consultants, but it is up to the client to independently approach the consultants and negotiate the terms and conditions of any resulting consultancy.

**Association of Fundraising Consultants: www.afc.org.uk**
Members of the AFC are accredited to the highest professional standards within the EU. Committed to advancing philanthropic endeavour, AFC members also subscribe to a rigorous code of ethics.

**EU Consult: www.euconsult.org**
EU Consult is a European network of senior ethically-minded consultants serving the not-for-profit sector.

**Institute of Fundraising: www.institute-of-funding.org.uk**
The IoF maintains an extensive list of consultants specialising in fundraising around a wide range of areas.

**Management Development Network: www.mdn.org.uk**
This is a network of experienced freelance consultants working in the voluntary sector. The site includes a list of its members and a breakdown by region and specialism. The directory is also available in hard copy.

**NAVCA: www.navca.org.uk**
NAVCA (National Association for Voluntary and Community Action) maintains two free online directories:
- a directory of 180 trainers and consultants with experience of working with the voluntary and community sector. Access is via a dedicated site, www.trainersandconsultantsdirect.org.uk

- a directory of recommended consultants capable of undertaking assignments dealing with procurement and competitive tendering. Access is via NAVCA's site: click 'strategic policy work' and then 'procurement' to find it.

**NCVO: www.ncvo-vol.org.uk**
NCVO publishes an online and print directory of approved consultants available free of charge to the voluntary and community sector.

**SETAS: www.setas.co.uk**
The Social Enterprise Training and support website contains an online directory of consultants specialising in social enterprise.

**VolResouce: www.volresource.org.uk**
This site lists a variety of consultants and consultancy resources. To access this, click on 'service providers' and then 'services index'.

## 2. Organisations hosting a consultancy network

The following organisations host consultancy networks. To secure the services of a consultant an approach will usually need to be made to the host organisation, which will then nominate one or more possible consultants from the network. Often the terms and conditions are set down by the host organisation.

**CAF: www.cafonline.org**
CAF manages a network of 50 consultants experienced in all areas of the charitable sector. Services range from quick organisational reviews to longer term assistance as in the case of mergers. CAF aims to put forward the consultant that best matches an organisation's needs.

**CAN: www.can-online.org.uk**
CAN acts as a broker between a number of consultants and community organisations involved in social enterprise.

**Community Matters: www.communitymatters.org.uk**
Community Matters runs two consultancy schemes:
- Community consultancy service: This utilises a team of trained community volunteers to provide advice and information on a range of core specialities. It is a low-cost scheme tailored to the needs of community organisations. Community Matters members get a free consultancy as part of their membership.

- Major consultancy service: This service utilises 40 professional consultants and is used by better resourced organisations for larger assignments.

**Neighbourhood Renewal Unit: www.neighbourhood.gov.uk**
The NRU runs a network of 150 associate Neighbourhood Renewal Advisers that help partnerships and communities (for example, New Deal For Communities, local strategic partnerships) involved in delivering neighbourhood renewal themselves. They include regeneration practitioners, service providers and residents.

**PrimeTimers: www.primetimers/org.uk**
PrimeTimers is a not-for-profit company created to help charity, voluntary and community groups grow and achieve their aims through the provision of cost-effective, business-inspired support and solutions. Its members are drawn from the commercial sector and it sources:
- interim and project managers, both full and part time
- high level mentors
- part-time specialists especially in strategic finance, marketing & HR
- small teams with a range of skills for a complex project
- candidates equipped to take on full-time permanent positions
- volunteers to undertake discrete projects

**Scarman Trust: www.thescarmantrust.org**
The Scarman Trust brokers consultancies through its regional offices to support the development of sustainable, scalable, adaptable and replicable social enterprises.

**Solace: www.solaceenterprises.com**
Solace Enterprises has 800 associates and provides a wide range of resourcing, executive development and consultancy services to all areas of the public sector.

**The Digbeth Trust: www.digbethtrust.org.uk**
The Digbeth Trust operates a professional and technical service for voluntary and community organisations in Birmingham and the West Midlands. It has a list of 40 accredited consultants and aims to match the client's requirements to the expertise of the consultant. It also assists potential clients in identifying their consultancy needs and drawing up their brief.

## 3. Organisations brokering pro bono assistance

**Business Community Connections: www.bcconnections.org.uk**
Business Community Connections provides a free online
resource centre for charities wishing to obtain support from
business. It is a good source of intelligence about pro bono assistance.

**IT4Communities: www.IT4communities.org.uk**
IT4 Communities is part of the ChangeUp ITC hub and hosts the
leading IT volunteering programme. Its main areas of activity
are:
- introducing skilled professional volunteers to voluntary
  and community sector organisations
- promoting volunteering among IT professionals and
  companies
- providing best practice resources on IT volunteering.

**LawWorks: www.lawworks.org.uk**
LawWorks is the operating name of the Solicitors Pro Bono
Group. It is an independent charity that supports, promotes and
encourages a commitment to pro bono assistance among solicitors. It runs a number of services including LawWorks For
Community Groups, which provides free advice on business law
to community groups.

**Pilotlight: www.pilotlight.org.uk**
Pilotlight works to help small innovative charities grow and fulfil
their potential. It does this by recruiting members from business
and industry, proven leaders and 'high fliers' who want to donate
their skills to charities. It matches these members with charities
that need to build their infrastructure and organisational
resources in order to survive and grow.

**Planning Aid: www.planningaid.rtpi.org.uk**
Planning Aid provides free independent and professional advice
and support on planning issues, to people and communities that
cannot afford to hire a planning consultant. In most UK regions
Planning Aid is run by the Royal Town Planning Institute.

**Professionals4Free: www.professionals4free.org.uk**
Professionals4Free is a signposting website with links to the
main brokers (for example, ProHelp) which, in turn, match
requests for help from voluntary sector organisations with offers
of pro bono (or in some cases subsidised) professional assistance. The site is managed by Business In The Community.

ProHelp: www.prohelp.org.uk
A national network of professional firms, co-ordinated by
Business In The Community, which undertake pro bono work for
voluntary organisations and community groups.

REACH: www.reach-online.org.uk
REACH recruits and supports volunteers with managerial,
professional and business experience who are then matched
with voluntary organisations needing part-time assistance.

The Cranfield Trust: www.cranfieldtrust.org
The Cranfield Trust offers free consultancy projects to charities
involved in addressing issues of poverty, disability or social
exclusion and uses a register of over 550 volunteers from the
commercial sector who give their time to act as free consultants.

The Media Trust: www.mediatrust.org
The Media Trust is a charity that works in partnership with the
media industry to build effective communications for the
charity and voluntary sector. Through its Media Match service,
organisations can register for advice from media and communications professionals.

Vital Spark Forum (VSF): www.v-s-f.org
VSF brings together philanthropic projects and skilled professionals. VSF actively selects charities that share its values and
helps them to identify challenges that could be overcome with
the assistance of professional services. VSF maintains a register
of skilled professionals who commit to volunteer some time to
projects that interest them.

Worshipful Company of Management Consultants (WCOMC):
www.wcomc.org.uk
WCOMC offers pro bono consulting and mentoring to chief
executives of London charities.

## 4. Trade bodies for consultants

These bodies provide a portal to their consultant members:
- The Institute of Business Advisers (www.iba.org.uk)
- The Institute of Management Consultancy
  (www.imc.co.uk)
- The Management Consultancies Association
  (www.mca.org.uk).

## 5. General online resources

**AskNCVO: www.ncvo.vol-org.uk/askncvo/**
NCVO's best practice resource for voluntary sector advice and information.

**Business Link: www.businesslink.co.uk**
Business Link is funded by the government's Small Business Service and provides guidance for new and small businesses. The website contains a very wide range of useful information about setting up and running an organisation in both the commercial and voluntary sectors. Business Link is also delivered on a local basis by a number of contractors working for the Small Business Service. Each of these runs its own website and provides a range of services including workshops and seminars.

**Community Matters: www.communitymatters.org.uk**
The Community Matters website is likewise a very useful resource.

**NAVCA: www.navca.org.uk**
NAVCA's website deals with a very wide range of information relating to the voluntary sector and running voluntary sector organisations.

**Regional voluntary sector umbrella bodies**
Regional umbrella bodies funded through the government's ChangeUp programme provide a wide range of local information and resources to the voluntary sector.

**VolResource: www.volresource.org.uk**
Volresource aims to provide quick and useful information on anything to do with running a voluntary sector organisation.

**Community and Voluntary Forum for the Eastern Region (COVER)**
www.cover-east.org

**North West Network**
www.nwnetwork.org.uk

**Regional Action West Midlands (RAWM)**
www.rawm.net

**Regional Action and Involvement South East (RAISE)**
www.raise-networks.org.uk

**South West Forum**
www.southwestforum.org.uk

**Third Sector Alliance (London)**
www.actionlink.org.uk/lvsc/Content.cfm?SubSiteContentID=98

**Voluntary Organisations Network North East (Vonne)**
www.vonne.co.uk

**Yorkshire and Humber Regional Forum**
www.yhregforum.org.uk